This is my horrific reminder of the unbelievable events that happened between my ex team East End Amateurs and Woodside amateurs. But lets got me there Me Steven Cameron started a football te al. After leaving Dyce juniors at the end of season 200 who has played in goals since he was a child. When h tournament called champion street in Aberdeen. Tha tournament. He was unlucky to get beat in the semi fi city Giants not sure what the script with that was as t ners. But he won super saves goalie of the tournamen

with me or my youngest brothers football careers. So on the day of the final that was played at Cove Rangers pitch. He was presented with his trophy from Scottish legend Alex McLeish.

<u>The Provest rust Pumas in the summer of 1993 and 4 of them ended up playing for the Royals</u>

Who we all know lifted many a trophy for Aberdeen FC including a European trophy back in 1983. Still the last Scottish club to win a European trophy so this was the summer of 1983.

So on the day of the final that was a proud day for me as I had trained and helped him become one of the best keepers in his age group yet he was picked for the primary school select and he got picked but was going to be sub so fucked them off as that used to be picked before the trials because I knew he was getting picked from one of the mangers of the select Alan Keith who ran his Middlefield boys club the team my brother had played for since he was aged 10.

But Alan who unfortunately is no longer with us but gone but not forgotten Alan Keith know as Biff was the type of man who just loved football he put a lot of effort running Middlefield boys club then he moved onto East End JFC and also the whole Aberdeen primary school football games he ran so you can see he was a passionate man for the great game that is football well when you win but Alan gave a lot of time in his short life to running kids football then due to his years of seeing young players he had a Middlefield team that went a few seasons unbeaten and won the juvenile Scottish cup when we was transitioning from the Royals Fc to East End Amateurs that preseason we played them in a friendly game they beat us 2-0 and they were only under 18s it was only a friendly game but they had some really good players buy they had played that long together hey knew their jobs and stuck to them and like when we were the Royals wining becomes a habit and we also had a squad of boys that all got along and were friends. But Biffs Middlefield team won the Scottish juvenile cup at under 15s season 2001/02 then the following season under 16s 2002/03 so that's some feat two win the national trophy two seasons on the trot just shows football in Scotland doesn't stop when you go over the Forth road bridge.

Alan Keith Middlefiled boys club, Rothes, EastEnd Jfc Aberdeen primary school secretary he lived for his wife kids and football sadly missed.

When Biff asked about signing my brother as the former manager had handed the rains over to Biff so he came and spoke with my parents at there home and was great with me and my brother even though he must of got sick of me at times as I just love to win and hate seeing people not trying. And I used to make it known so you could imagine. I meant well never did I ever argue with him in all the time I knew him. So that's how I first met Alan Keith RIP.

Alex McLiesh   And the World football legend Himself

So Scott was presented with his trophy from Scottish legend Alex McLeish. Beating Real Madrid in extra time with former Middlefield boys club player John Hewitt scoring the winning goal So that was a rememberable day.

Aberdeen Legend Alex McLiesh Him and Willie Miller played there whole careers together at one club Aberdeennow that sort of thing will never happen again.

John Hewitt scoring Aberdeen's most important goal in there hisrtory

And how could you ever forget this man well Aberdeen's people in power did Aberdeen Legend John Hewitt scorer of the 1983 wining goal against the mighty Real Madrid yet he never was included in Aberdeen's Centenary year, Pure liberty fact.

He was a product of the same team my brother played boys club football Middlefield boys club, this man was Ole Gunner Solskjaer before he was even born great penalty box player, and has scored for his home town club in a European cup final winner against Real Madreid that's the thing you really now could only dream of but he achieved his dream and the whole of the town as there wasn't much Rangers and Celtic fans in Glasgow never mind Aberdeen fact people if everyone supported the home town club or even go watch a junior game where you will get a beer and no fools hassling you about a silly song about tatties is not going to get you 6 months behind bars, and if you really think there was a shortage of tattie that's a lie there like weeds the grow and grow so don't listen to the mainstream media there full of it all fear from that lot.

This culture we live in today where everything is geared towards making people think its good to STICK in people FOR FANS SINGING THE SAME NONSENSE BACK yet the people in charge want you to grass up your fellow supporters years ago life was not like they make it out, things were better the game was better the working man could afford to watch there team with there kids but who is going to pay to watch a game in the freezing cold when there scared to say anything now that could offend someone and your jailed for something that's forgotten as soon as the fans leave the stadium.

But the way the world is heading its going to the Middle east all your best players fighters the lot will all be getting watched there as they don't scare there citizens about Covid plus there's loads of cash and that's all that matters now in sport or in life in general people go where the cash is and in the next 5 years all your major events are in the Middle east. As TV deals alone will not pay the top stars there wages because the reason Tyson Fury and am a convicted Nigerian failed Olympic boxing team for his home country as he sees Nigeria as his country or he wouldn't have tried out for the Olympic boxing team in 2008 I am Anthony 100 hours community service for having 10oz of herbal cannabis in his boot Joshua

Me iv never had a drugs conviction in my life yet this Nigerian drug dealer come iv changed my life around and am a roll model for kids why is a drug dealer the pin up man of boxing yet my mothers a traveler and none of my mothers family have drug charges but if they were to tell people they were travelers instantly people think your out to rob them yet the government that you all rely on are worse than any gypsies and that's a fact. Well enough about politics back to the beautiful game that is football and my money is on Fury worse beating that Wilder got.

Fury stops Joshua 8th round.

The reason am speaking about boxing is because up until my oldest daughter was born when I was 21 years old I done both from a young age as you needed to be able to look after yourself where am from but I had so much energy I could sit at piece and the boxing training and the football training both after I had done a days work so I was as fit as a butchers dog at that age.

But I had to make a choice and well as you will read I sometimes took money when it was offered there's not one team iv signed for and asked how much that's not me I want to know the manager and the club are all sing from the same song sheet otherwise its not for me I get anxiety and feel like punching players over the shit they moan about and am playing because I loved football.

But honestly there's been loads of times at training and at games I felt like punching a few boys over the years but even though iv held myself back because I then remove myself from these people as I used to hit first then ask questions due to my impulsive behaviors but iv never fought at junior level as when I was younger the referees protected you a bit better than the referees in the lower levels as there working there way up the ranks.

But I had to make the choice as iv said as work boxing football and work add a newborn baby girl so I bought a punch bag and kept playing football and as you will read in this, just as well I can look after myself.

My younger brother Scott played for Middlefield boys club and then stopped playing basically but he then started playing and helping me and enjoyed playing again as most of my players in the Royals FC team I played and managed was built with players that stopped playing but my brother and myself plus a few of the Royals players had all played with junior teams ie Dyce Juniors, Hermes, Banchory, Lewis United, East End FC, ParkvaleJFC, Cruden bay JFC,

Cunninstone United JFC, Hall Russell United JFC and as you will read all them teams wanted to sign him and between me and him we have played for all that junior clubs.

Yet both of us and these other players gave up on junior football for one reason or another and I gave them game time every week nearly and got a lot of them there confidence back and showed they were more than capable of playing at that level no problem. After East End my brother signed for banchory he was playing weekly and playing well but had to leave Banchory ST due to all the fuel he was going through with training out there twice a week when your driving a Subaru Wrx you'll understand.

Middlefield Primary School after being bombed in April 1943.

My Middlefield Milk cup 7 aside team we should of won it but got beat on corners in the semi

He's played for Dyce juniors a lot he played anytime they needed him even when he was signed for the Royals Fc as we played Sunday's so just goes to show the quality of the squad we had that due to my long term friendship with there manager Andy Milne who got Dyce Juniors promoted to the super league for the first time in there history and as you will read later we played them the season before they won the 1st division and they ended that season 4th th.

Me Steven Gordon Cameron I was born in July 1976 started off playing for my Primary School team Middlefield after my uncle Donald who played for Montrose and had trials with St Mirren but ended up getting Married as his Girlfriend was pregnant with twin girls so back then football was like it is now the wages weren't that great so he got a job in the oil and gave up playing as his family came first. But it was him who first showed me how to play he would spend hours showing me how to control and pass the ball so Mr wood the school headmaster noticed me playing in the play ground and asked me to go to the school team training.

And before I knew it I was substitute aged 9 for the school first team because the class sizes were a lot more like there was two classes of children when I went right through primary school so the school had a B team but I was put straight into the first team. But ever since I can remember iv always doubted myself ability, due to lack of self confidence yes people me I felt like that. Due to the brutality of other children can be saying things to make you doubt yourself which sticks in your head as that would only spur me more to be better, but I knew even at a young age if people were having a go at you when you were a child it was them coping with there own issues like jealousy because you were better than them in whatever it was you were doing people. If others are haters it's due to them being jealous as it's a fact of life but you don't realise it till your older and wiser.

Middlefield Primary School below

My First Ever football medal I received showing my age

But even as a child I suffered bad from anxiety meeting new people was difficult due to lack of trusting others due to the area I was brought up in where you could trust anyone people, and it was rough and I had to learn from my early years how to look after yourself back then society was totally different if you never fought back you would just get bullied all the time so I had many a fight being brought up in Middlefield I would beat one and another would come all until I had fought and beat them all and I wasnt one that looked for toruble as you will read as you read on you will get the picture.

But I carried on playing and a other thing was the fact I lived in Aberdeen and stayed at the time and probably still is one of its most deprived areas Middlefield even though my mothers house was clean and fresh and we stayed on the very border of the real poverty but me and both my bothers had all the latest things and I now know that was the reason I got grief these others never had these materialistic things that mean nothing really but that's life. I still got grief for living In that area that's another thing I never let it get me down or stop me so here's a bit of advice never let bullies put you down you just stand up to them but that's another book. But in the end I never failed due to me not trying,

I failed because other wanted me to fail fact. At football and in adult life but am still here writing this book thankfully after a Horrific car crash in my fathers car traveling North of Aberdeen to his home in Kingseat Aberdeenshire when a women in a Saab came head on after fish tailing on a bad wet corner and the police estimated the impact at 110mph so both of us sustained serious injuries as you would think in such a terrible crash.

Am not calling it an accident as she was charged and delt with by the court system but I broke my back in 4 places and fractured my L5 vertebra my spine for people not so clued up on the ins and outs of medical language so I have no feeling in my left leg and my left pinky knuckle snapped in half and the air bag broke my nose. As iv said both me and my father were lucky to be here so this story I thought would take some of my time up as am physically properly disabled due to the crash plus am suffering PTSD which iv found writing therapeuticall it helps take my mind of the crash even though as I write this iv goose pimples.

The Ball that every kid in the world wanted after watching these football's in Italy 90.

My father had bought me an Addais's tango from bridge streets <u>Crombie sports,</u>

He warned me not to even bounce it on the concrete as back then it was a expensive ball used in Italy 90.

I don't need to tell you what happened the first time that I was allowed to take it into the Middlefield school field where all the local kids that played football wanted a game so we could play with the coveted Tango. So after a lot of arguing your sides better than ours for awhile as you all reading this will remember this carry on as a child.

Mind you I have seen it at a few junior clubs iv been at. So the game starts and then the local group that couldn't play the simple game of football so thought they would bully others that did, so they tried taking the ball and this was when I knew I was able to play football plus fight. I remember my middle brother saying run well I had enough of the same people bullying the whole area for ages till that day they tried to steal the Adidas Tango and I tangoed with the leader of the pack and left him in a bad way.

But least I went home with my football and see what was weird my father smiled more when my brother was telling him all the details he looked so proud. Yet I could score a hatrick and come home smiling from ear to ear and he never took any notice. Back then I thought he carried more about my fighting and boxing than football. He very rarely came to watch my games but he showed me from a young boy how to live off the land though. We would spend hours fishing the rivers Dee and Don.

Iv spent hours of my life fishing that part of the river iv had some good fish out of that pool The biggest salmon iv caught on the river Dee the Maryculter beat. Took me 45 minutes to reel it in he helped me land this fish as I was tiered at only 15. Iv had a 7 pound sea trout in my opinion one of the nicest trout to eat. Tinfoil with Garlic butter little sea salt bobs your uncle lovely fish supper. Also caught a 5lb wild Brown trout on a worm when you could use them legally on the rivers which are fly only now.

We would go haring with the dogs or have a few ferrets and polecats for putting down the rabbit holes so if Tesco's closed tomorrow I could give advice on hunting for food to eat not waste. So back to my father and my football the whole problem was he couldn't play the game and never understood the ins and outs of the sport so he's told me he never came due to not wanting to look stupid if asked about how the game rules got into the conversation. As he's the type of person that has to know exactly what he's speaking about.

<u>Sunnbank juniors pitch Heathryfold Park not looking its best there but its a great surface to play on with a standing capacity of 2200.</u>

The old badge you bought and your mother stitched it on as you will see do some research on the club its sad that there gone the ground is houses now not sure if the junior pitch is still there but they still have the center in Tillydrone though so you never know they could make a come back in the juniors one day.

Aberdeen Lads club former player Mark Perry made the Aberdeen first team.

I starting playing for Middlefield Primary School aged 9 as I said and played upfront. Iv also played age 10yrs old on Sunnybank Juniors pitch Heathrlyfold park, I remember it well as when your just a young boy the local junior club is like playing at a senior clubs ground so that was the first time I played there is a good memory to look back on now, as how excited I was to be getting the chance to play on a pitch that was huge when your ten and its not much smaller when your an adult, me i was able to go past people and was very quick and could score goals.

So the more I played the local Aberdeenshire Juvenile teams started to take notice and it wast soon before they came calling and after getting a phone call and back then it was house phones no fancy mobiles in those days. Unless you lived in London and working in the financial sector. So house call it was from one of the best juvenile clubs Aberdeen Lads Club.

But the week before I had just trained twice with Seafield swift's and had promised to return to training but the Lads Club was a big juvenile club. See as a kid football was my escape from not the best home life plus the fact of where I was from so I would play from the minute I woke up till the minute I went to slepp football was all I thought about because it takes away the thoughts of feeling the odd one out all the time the players at Seefield were all from posh well to do places and I really felt nerve's even been dropped off at a place beside the rubislaw quarry. See what you have to understand my mother really though that I was going to have a lot better up bring than she had so she was want me to go with Seafield.

Who then end up being sponsored by MTM construction who then went on to fund Culter juniors with players that I would of played with had I choice to stay at that club through my juvenile career but I really felt out of place there and they made me feel really want and everyone was nice but it was just how I felt at the time plus weren't as established as at the time the ALC was well maintained and was close to my home.

Also had a training center in Tillydrone in Aberdeen plus there was kids there that i knew through either through family or friends staying in the Tillydrone area so i wasnt as nerves going along there as i knew i would have the same intrests and speak the same and that they were rougher kids who werent as they would react scared or hadnt seen that sort of passion for players not trying or doing something stupid even though they knew i would have mad out bursts or arguing with other players as you do especially when your a kid.

So the coaches the whole Aberdeen Lads club suited me better than if i had been round about them for any lenght of time because i gave my all as a kid in games and most when i was an adult and would have crazy out bursts i couldnt help i would even go off on one with yself if i done something wrong and knew i could of and should of done better and seriuosly had i stayed they would of ended up throughing me out of there team or made me feel proper unconfortable and tolarated my behaviour only because i was better than the players they had at that time.

So me going to the Lads club was a better chioce for me but my mother really wanted to stay at Seafield as she had her own cleaning business and no disrespect to anyone at the Lads club the parents that were invovled had money and this is only my thoughts looking ack she thought that if i played for Seafield she might get some business contracts wido she is lol.

But no my mother helped raise money for the Lads Club through her business contacts in the end she even organised a jumble sale that raised i think £1200 which helped the club teams my mother liked doing things like that as her business was going well and i think that money went towards the trip to Isle of Wight.

So with the Lads club we were under 12s and the team traveled by bus to the Isle of White for a tournament against teams from all over I remember getting on a hovercraft from Southampton there and I was only 12 was a mad experience but it was a long bus trip.

The games were OK but was an all round great experience i will never forget as I was saying we played a team and this was an under 12 or 13 can't remember but one of there players had a beard no joke. But that was a great experience playing against players from all over the UK and it was the first time I was away from my mother and father.

This is how I was treated by my father he never came to the ALC Tillydrone center to wave good bye when your young little things like that make you think does he even want me to play football. I remember my mother was there she was all emotional seeing her 12 year old boy away with a load of strangers miles away but everyone involved were totally professional well they tried but when you have kids like me running about there's defiantly going to be something happen.

Well sorry to tell you we fought with the players from the other teams because they were all English and we got the jock throw at us so with 2 shandy's it all kicked of and I don't mean on the pitch this was in these old style butlins shallys total dump but funny to get away from Aberdeen and to be playing against other teams even though some of teams had kids about under 15s but all a great life experience.

Well years on I ended up being the manager of my former primary school team Middlefield due to my oldest daughter putting my name forward. Due to the team not having a manager the team was going to fold. So I took charge of the school team. They had a very good team with kids that could play. So me and Charlie Masson who's son Russell played so Charlie helped out with trying to control these crazy kids but they knew when not to mess about as I am a winner and if the school team done shit I would see that as a reflection of myself.

So I would take the training and children don't need to work to much on fitness well back even that short time ago there was at least 16-18 kids fit enough out of one P6 class and one P7 so the children would not work much on fitness a 10-15 minute warm up drills then work on making them all comfortable on the ball that was one of the first things I went and bought was a ball each for them at training.

Well back then that team of kids were all fit So I worked on getting them organised and would work on positions and back then it was 11 aside. So as I said I would work on drills more about being in position as a team. And through the season the kids all got to know what there job was. And i always worked on the things they done well rather than deflate there confidence by telling them the things they were bad as some of these kids was all they had heard from people in there family's so I always keep there home life in my head if they were upset about things so I would be working on there things they are good at and there smiling then you can incorporate drills that you introduce little by little as there children and some take longer to develop and some don't have the attention span then your training session ends up just a rabble so as iv said get to know your players best attribute.

Then work on drills that will develop the things they don't like or want to do as there children and like myself not all children have good self belief in there own ability so will shy away from trying to learn new things incase they get slagged off from there team mates but as long as the kids are playing with a smile on there face you will get there attention be honest and explain yourself properly so they all understand what each other are good at. Like at the end of every training and games I would speak about the good things each player from goalkeeper to substitute at training I would always pick a point in the game when each player done something good and because they were winning and smiling why disrupt the harmony. If you have a kid 6 ft who can't real play the game that well but is willing to listen and learn. Because they all want to be Lionel Messi.

Well if that kid can tackle but isn't good at heading yet he's 6ft. You work with him or (her) on heading and defending. It's not hard to work on positions and work with what you have and play week in week out until they understand what they are good at, and then make them always do what they've been taught and showed in the simplest form possible football really inst a difficult game the whole aim is win but with a bit of class,

Plus you need players that are able to listen and learn your way you want the game played, me I like attacking with a sitting midfield player alongside a box to box midfielder and pace at both full backs and wide midfielder players that can get crosses in the box and the only positions that size is a problem is Goalkeeper and center half the rest of the team as long as there strong and can play then I would pick a player who's 5ft that can benefit my style of play to having a 6-5ft boy that's no use with the ball at there feet as dribbling as is heading and tackling an art.

The season progressed well the kids all jelled and they won the Emsily cup beating St Joseph's RC School, Aberdeen 2-0. After that game iv never been so discussed by so called Catholics calling children degrading names because they came from one of Aberdeen's most deprived areas still to this day its one of the roughest areas but I really couldn't believe my ears with fully grown men calling a 10-11 year old he was a Minker.

The New School Manor Park.

But a minker with a winners medal and me coming from travelers from my mothers side iv seen all this not racism but discrimination my mothers seen a lot more of that as a child growing up as a gypsie girl shes had it over her lifetime and doesn't even let some people know shes of traveler stock and I think that's where I get my temper from but if people read and buy this just apart of my life then I will write another as iv lived a colourful life just to say the least so in 2005 you have people of God being totally horrible to children and I hate children being hurt.

CUP CRACKERS: Middlefield captain Aiden Taylor proudly displays the Emslie Cup with his victorious team-mates.

<u>The last Middlefield Primary School team to win that trophy as the school has been rebuilt and renamed so that class of kids there all over achieved in that great season they had you know you've got it right when parents are not moaning all the time.</u>

Which isn't the kids fault but it never bothered them that day because they were walking away with winners medals and big smiles on there face. They were also runners up in the league 2 to Dyce primary school which was a great feat as the class sizes and how many Primary 6 and 7 classes the school has and back then they never included the number of girls but didnt the head Mistress count the girls so the team were placed in league 2 rather than 3.

With the quality of players in the spine of the team we would of probably won league 3 as the kids only lost the league by one point,

I was really proud not for myself but for the kids that listened and learned and got a trophy for there effort. And they will go down in history as the last team to put Middlefield schools name on the cup as the school got knocked down after being bombed during war times and a nice Granite building and now its a kit school that will be lucky if its still standing in 30 years time called Manor Park. End of the day that's all that matters playing sports all this taking part nonsense is why the Scotland team have taken a million years to qualified for a Major tournament.

As society has gotten to soft and children are so tuned into technology that there getting fat with the things there putting in the food chain and vaccines and basically children are to lazy fact, That's the reason iv added the times I spent with my father doing hunting and these are skills lacking in the whole of society today the people who make the decisions want a society that's totally dependent on them supplying the masses with some real bad food things so there needs to be people questioning things more and start supporting your local butchers and farm shops as you just need to look at the diet of some children and obesity in both adults and children but its a thing I feel passionate about.

You need to be blind if you cant see the link between the junk food society we live in and also here in Scotland Heart attacks are the biggest killer but all these medical problems are due to the Scottish drinking culture as we have an excuse to drink anytime and its probably Scotland's biggest problem that the SNP haven't even tried to sort the problem, if they think upping the price of alcohol has made any difference well there very very wrong.

Remember I haven't done one SFA coaching children's or adults courses that they have blue printed years ago and have tried all sorts of grass roots changes to the size of the teams to the size of the pitches and known of these have manged until the last few years that we as a nation are lucky we have a decent generation of footballers playing at a high level so that's had a knock on affect to the national side.

But what the SFA allowed to happen to the Scottish league with all these small clubs trying to compete with the likes of Celtic and Rangers as they had players like Gascoigne Laudrup Larrson Lubomir Moravcik Hately Butcher the list goes on but in with that mixer there was Scottish Talent still playing along side these top players then the prices started going up with the start of the English Premiership in 1992 they inflated wages and as I say they quality of these foreign players that were on huge wages clubs like Dundee for example they had Fabrizio Ravaneill who only played 5 games in a whole season.

Then things just went from bad to worse as even big clubs like the both Glasgow giants having there problems with flops but they had the financial clout to take a few hits well as we all know Rangers weren't paying the tax man as they were keeping up with Celtic and chasing European success as was the whole of the Scottish football tried even the small clubs Dundee, Aberdeen, Dundee Untied, Hearts, Hibs Motherwell all these clubs stop a whole generation of young scottish players get first tea experience even if they were maybe not as experianced but had same ability weren't getting the time in the first team due to have these well over priced foreign players as iv said thats what killed the scotland team we were at one point if your granny had went to see the Loch Ness monster you qualified for Scotland proper joke and it was the SFA as much as the clubs all greed as was proved in the end.

But then you had players of class as iv said and here are some of the greats and flops iv been lucky enough to have seen play live at Pittodrie stadium when I wasn't playing football myself and I cant say I support Aberdeen as iv always played football on a Saturday but when big games are on and I get a free complementary seat with drinks before and halftime bites to eat and more free drinks in the legends lounge in the Richard Donald stand named after the long serving board member and I would like to that Neil Stewart of <u>Ram Tubulars</u> for taking me to that Rangers game was not a bad night as they gave you more free drink after and I think I drank and stayed a lot longer as I was speaking with the players but I enjoyed the night Neil so thanks again and since iv gave you a great bit of advertisement am looking for a whole box and dont worry about the drinks bill as am sober apart from all these meds am on.

Gascoigne

Larrson

Moravcik

£1 Million FLOP

All clubs were paying wages they couldn't afford and then because they had spent so much on transfers and wages they had no choice but to play these flops ahead of Young Scottish players and that's what the problem was not the grass roots it wasn't broken it broke due to all premier league teams buying foreign players hoping they could sell them on for a profit to the bigger clubs,

But at the end of the day its took well over two decades for the clubs to recover and are giving young player like Scotland captain Andrew Robertson a chance to go through these development academies these clubs were forced to do and look for Scottish young players and give them 1st team experience, so iv coached myself and played the game the way iv been brought up watching it and also remembering all the bad things managers iv played for have done and learned from there mistakes and the biggest thing of all being able to see the best qualities.

Other people have and get the best out of them on the field by giving praise when players young or old have done well even in defeat if there doing whats asked of them given time these players get better as iv said you praise the good stuff while all the time trying to improve them on the things they think because of there other experiences with former coaches managers or whoever has told them there no good well if you hear that time after time it sticks in your head and I don't even mean sports

 I just mean even in the work place or home could be anything or anyone who has got it into your head that you aren't good enough or you cant do that I use that as motivation to stride to always prove people wrong I know through my life iv also tried to prove myself over and over to different people just to show I was able to do what in my head people were thinking I wasn't able to do due to having serious self doubt issues in my head. So even in my personal life I thought like that so what am trying to get at is don't ever let anyone tell you your no good at this or that use that energy that it gives you inside to go on to prove yourself worthy simple you either strive to be the best YOU can be at anything your good at and enjoy but life is a struggle and you need to stay strong through the good times and the bad plus timing in life is everything as some are luckier than you doesn't mean there better, they are if they are totally dedicated and you are just wasting the talent at whatever your doing and have ability to be at the top but you need to have the talent in the first place.

Be the most hard working you possibly can be and its really true practice makes perfect and hard work and living the life and not sitting in a park with your friends drinking and taking drugs as a child or as an adult drinking everyday in the pub.

Or get a chance and take drugs even if you think its only a recreational little bit here and there it will ruin everything in your life never mind sport or work, I know as I went down that road. I took drink drugs fighting at different times in life when I was basically going about in self destruct mode as a child and at times in my adult life where iv self medicated with illegal drugs never heroin but iv also used steroids to train as I was getting older and they fuck with your head.

Along with other drugs its not good but iv always worked, the times when iv been bad is when things in life aren't going good like when iv had serious injuries and me being hyper and iv boundless energy at times I would self medicate with drink and drugs.

But everyone has bad times in life you need to come back and prove the haters and doubters wrong I swear the more that I think people are thinking am unable to do something I always try my best to come back a even better person from the bad times as iv had many through my life believe me a lot worse than this football stories as just like my football life as you will read on and make your own mind up if am a thug or just a person who god has put on this earth to just keep over coming adversity.

And even if you don't believe in god iv not had any help in my life apart from my family the help I have had is from people that understand me and know deep down I would try helping anyone to get on in this life, as if you know me then you will know what am saying is true another problem in my life am to nice at times and that's the truth as you will read when others aren't so nice when it comes to telling stories to the police but as iv said that's for another day.

So after leaving Middlefield Primary I joined Harlaw Academy in 1st year I was picked out of a whole year of kids that had all played together and knew each other from being at the same primary schools and they never liked the fact that I was picked and I could of played upfront because at the trials I played upfront and there was one game the goalkeeper got injured in one of the games and I went in goal for the rest of the game and pulled off some great saves as I used to learn my bro so I knew how to play basically every position on the park as all I studied was football night and day and with me having OCD I always take things I enjoy doing seriously and let it be known when am annoyed.

But at Harlaw the other kids tried bulling me because of the area I was from and other non-sense and I ended up getting expelled for fighting that's why I ended up at St Machar. So I played in goals for them as they never had a keeper and I could play in goal as I had on occasions for Lads Club if we never had a goalkeeper and I was like a cat as you will read later on I played a few games in goals twice against Dyce Juniors in a 1-1 draw and there goal came from a penalty. Second game ended 3-3 and Andy Moule was playing upfront for Dyce JFC after being released by Dundee United.

So after not even over a year at that secondary school I was expelled and then went to St Machar Academy where I knew most of the other pupils as I stayed in the same area. But looking back now my mother just thought she was doing her best for me at the time. But I was a year too Old for the St Macher School team and they had a great team in the lower age group but all were in my classes.

But that team consisted of Kevin Morgan who was at Aberdeen also Kevin Chiriste Grieg Topp at Dundee United also Andy Moule who went to Hazlehead Academy who is now a friend of many years. Who got a game for united but got ended up released and I remember playing against him when he was at Dyce JFC and I was at Cumminestone drew 3-3 so he had a fall from big time stuff playing in the Scottish premier leagues to Dyce Juniors, well we all pure messed up for one reason or another.

My Mothers street where iv played under the street lights for hour on end.

Kevin Morgan representing Scotland in Holland

Kevin Christie ended up full time at Aberdeen and then Alex McLeish paid £10k to take him to Motherwelll.

Former class mates Kevin Christie and Morgan great goalkeeper released by Aberdeen due to him only being 5-10".

So at St Macher I was playing only juvenile due to St Macher not having a team for me due to the August birth date back then the players mentioned were all in my year at school but played in the age group bellow me as I missed the cut off date by 9 days pure unfair as a year when your a child is a big difference in physical side to the game but I never let it bother me and still enjoyed my football. As I was saying about the Lads club which is still there but unfortunately the club pitches have been sold except the Aberdeen lads club juniors pitch the last time I looked before my car crash.

The Aberdeen Lads Club Jameison Park total mess

As a youngster if the groundsman George caught you on the grass he would chase you off instantly as he really did take care off all the pitches, The last time I visited the pitch it broke my heart to see it in such a bad state.

The groundsman George would cry look at the state of the hole grail of the Aberdeen Lads club the reason I signed was because I wanted to play on the Junior pitch which I did but not for them plus after me being there since 10 I left due to the new manager as he ruined the club to be honest here's me that's played most of my youth football at there juvenile club yet I ended up scoring against them at 17 while my former team mates were playing under 18s for there juvenile set up, its such a shame that miss management could cause probably one of the oldest youth set ups in the city of Aberdeen go to the wall but that man was dedicated to his groundsman job.

Well after a signing at age 10 I left either after under 15/16 not sure but I was watching the semi final between my brothers team Provost rust pumas and Girdlness Gunners who won 4-0 they never turned up that night but that's football.

That's the night watching my younger brother at champion street and i got talking to a man called Andy Milne who ran a junior team called Cuminestone United for people that don't know where it is well 6 miles from Turriff.

I went along to a friendly game for his team I scored a hatrick and after the game Andy couldn't wait to sign me and me not knowing nothing much about junior football other than my local junior Scottish cup winners Sunnybank and the Aberdeen Lads club juniors, so aged 16 I signed a pro form for at the time one of 5-6 worst teams in the North Region Junior football league.

Stephen Glass

My first season playing junior was an experience but I still scored goals most weeks and learned early how to look after yourself on a football pitch against fully grown men and back then the game was different you were allowed to jump in two footed tackles without even getting booked sometimes depending on the referee.

Iv played against in season 2 in junior football Stephen Glass who Aberdeen sold to English premiership Newcastle United for £750k he played 112 first team games for Aberdeen's first team from 1994-98 but was farmed out to junior football club Crombie Sports he then played on loan in season 1994-95 he then played 42
Stephen Glass.

first team games for Newcastle United between 1998-2001 and collected 1 full Scotland cap also played over 70 times for Watford and over 80 first team games for Hibernian in the Scottish premiership so its fair to say he went down a completely different paths as you will read the only thing we have in common in football is we both went into management as he is currently manager of Atlanta United 2 who play there football in the USL 2.

He club he was farmed out to Crombie sports who are no longer in junior football along with Cumminestown United, Inverurie Juniors, Inch juniors Inverurie Juniors pitch is now in the hands of feeder club to the Highland Inverurie Loco works who joined up with juvenile club Colony Park to form up and joined the junior football League .

Then you have the teams that have left the juniors to go Highland league. The standard of junior football not just in Aberdeenshire but in Scotland as a whole is not anywhere near the standard it was in the 90s and the early 00s that's what iv seen. And with the pyramid system in place the junior game will die if the don't go with the times because clubs with better facility's than league clubs are going to try getting into the Scottish league proper just look how well Cove Rangers are doing in the seniors since stepping up from the Highland league also Edinburgh city from the lowlands league .

But I did enjoy my football at Cumminestone even though they got beat most weeks least I was playing every week against men when really I was just a kid who should of been playing 2 season at under 18s but instead was scoring goals for the bottom club in junior football.

Cuminestone United Juniors Pitch.
Hit the net a Few times on that pitch

See what would make me laugh all these monkeys that would stand with a tie and shirt on and claim to have played junior football me personally I don't do sub unless the managers got a valid reason.

And the best pitch I played on in the juniors was Turriff United's ground is like a bowling green as you see.

Turriff United stand built since moving up to the Highland League.

Kilbirnie Ladeside Junior Football Ground Capacity 1000.

One of the most hostile games I played in the juniors was against Kilbirnie Ladeside from Ayrshire they weren't very hospitable to us sheep Shaggers and during the warm up the kids were throwing fireworks from behind the goal at us so at the time was defiantly a bit of a eye opener as there huge crowd kept chanting none stop at the time I was 17 year old and was a bit scared to be honest never showed it but still scored a goal and for once I never even celebrated was shitting myself but what an experience teams there in the late 90s were getting crowds of well over a few thousand for big derby games.

That day they said there was 249 people because in junior football back then not sure if it's still the same now. But in the junior Scottish cup if the crowds over 250 you get some of the gate money. Now that day the whole side of there stand was full and even police there yet they said there was 249 fans there lol. But playing in games like that can only make you a better player.

My second season at Cuminestone United I scored 15 Goals which is disputed by manager Andy Milne who says 14 but 14 or 15 is a good return from a 18 year old kid playing against some really good players back then as iv said Aberdeen Football club would farm the youth players out to junior clubs and just look at Stephen Glass he went on and had a great career and played a season or less for Junior club Crombie Sports.

Also Craig Ireland played for Parkvale he went to to play in the seniors and again playing against physically stronger players makes you better no shadow of a doubt there. Plus that season we had a few players from Fraserburgh and they knew Fraserburgh Highland league side manager Charlie Duncan true story.

He watched me against Maud and I had played well and scored so that season this was the one and only time I had ever been substitute for Cuminsetone and surprise surprise who was it against Fraserburgh United juniors who play up at either the School or Collage but I remember sitting in the dressing room and Andy read out the team I thought what you read that out wrong but no he made me substitute I had no clue this Highland league club was looking on take me on for a trial.

Fraserburgh Highland League Ground Capacity 480 seat total 3000.

The manager Charlie Duncan had came to watch the game and see me yet am sitting on a bench for the only time ever so I later found out from the Fraserburgh boys so make your own mind up on that one.

Russsell Anderson

So any Aberdeen's coaching staff if your reading maybe bring that back never done that pair any harm. Plus there was more but am getting older people so can't remember everyone but that's the ones I remember playing against at junior level who had decent careers Russell Anderson played at Dyce Juniors before stepping up to the Aberdeen squad then made his first start in 1996 playing 280 games and scoring 18 goals before moving on to Sunderland for one million Stirling.

He played 1 game he is probably [Sunderlands 2nd worst signing only behind the ten million payed for Adam Johnson a convicted Pedophile who the club continued to play while they knew he was being investigated by the police have a look into that story] so he became a first team regular so in my opinion the junior game was a lot tougher than it is now as you read this there's not one junior player good enough to step up from the juniors to the Scottish premiership and Anderson even collected 16 under 21 caps from 97-99 remember he was playing junior the season before and he also gained 11 full Scotland caps yet he started off playing junior at the same time as I was playing but I was playing in the super league with Hall Russells so honestly cant remember playing against him he now is assistant manager at Formartine United.

Against Parkvale when Ireland was playing I scored in a 4-1 defeat and he was a big donkey but that's what clubs think makes a good player they can work with just because they have physical attributes it's crazy. So couldn't have been that bad that he couldn't stop me from scoring against his side.

So after two seasons playing junior football and having collected some great experience playing against teams with good players and having done well. The club folded.
At Cumminestone United there was no pressure on me and to be honest I done what I liked but never took the piss as iv respect and loyalty to the people I believe I think are worth such trust.

In two seasons I played on Inverurie Loco Works pitch scored in a 4-1 defeat but I played well with my old Adidas copa mundial and world cups in the winter. there was one game I remember was playing for Cuminnestone I broke one of the Inverurie Loco Works midfield player Jim Findlays jaw I never meant it I caught him with my arm as I was running away from him, because I turned basically I used my arms and upper body to keep the ball and he came of worse but genuinely I never meant it but he ended up worse off. He was a good player but that was years ago but am sure he remembers me well I think iv already apologised but if your reading this then here you go that's my apology.

But i got the chance to play week in week out and learned more in that two seasons playing than warming a bench somewhere or even worse not getting a strip at all which I could never get my head round the fact players would rather do that on a Saturday than play week in week out at a team who maybe wont be winning everything but your getting 90 minutes.

All these games when we would get thrashed and that would only happen when we played super league teams , sometimes getting some heavy defeats but I would rip Maud Crombie sports , Inch , Inverurie juniors , Formartine United, who in season two I played out my skin and we got a 0-0 draw but I missed a few sitters that day and Hall Russell who came runners up that season drew 2-2 with Inverurie juniors and Cuminestone ended up joint bottom with Inverurie JFC both clubs on 11 points.

DIVISION I

Dyce Jun	1	Inach	2
Formartine	0	Cuminestown	0
Inv Juniors	2	Hall Russell	2
Maud	0	Banchory St T.	3

	P	W	D	L	F	A	Pt
Longside	26	20	3	3	73	28	63
Hall Russell	26	17	7	2	47	24	58
Crombie	26	16	5	5	58	22	53
Hermes	26	15	6	5	83	33	51
Banchory St T.	26	12	9	5	63	32	45
Ellon Utd	26	13	2	11	50	38	41
Lads' Club	26	12	5	9	49	37	41
Fraserbrgh U	26	12	4	10	52	38	40
Formartine	26	8	6	12	44	46	30
Inach	26	8	6	12	47	57	30
Dyce Jun	26	5	4	17	31	65	19
Maud	26	5	3	18	32	59	18
Inv Juniors	26	2	5	19	31	77	11
Cuminestown	26	2	5	19	22	129	11

The Final League League table season 1994/95 Division one and I missed a sitter in the last game of the season to get them off the foot of the league table for the first time in years but still not bad for a 18 year old kid.

As you can read even the local paper reporter gave me it stinking for missing a sitter against Formartine JFC that would of got the club of the bottom of the league for the first time in 3 seasons. But we still had a decent season drew twice with Dyce 1-1 and 3-3 and both games I played in goals. Inverurie JFC 1-1 and 2-0 scored the three Inch 1-1 scored Maud 4-0 I ripped them to bits scored two and my old striking partner got two that night as well remember I smashed a free kick from 25 yards out and it hit the top corner.

So think I turned up when it matter against the clubs round about the same standard yet I still got goals in cup games against the bigger junior clubs. Plus I got to play on some great pitches and if your reading this and saying he was shit and he played for a shit team well at least I held my own against fully grown men back in a time when you could tackle properly without being sent off. Believe me am suffering from injuries yet but nothing like what am experiencing now.

So after two seasons I had spent with the club they folded and I was a bit gutted to be truthful but they were struggling too get 11 players on the park on some midweek games, but as Iv said I was actually winning them games so the ended up with a hardcore support of 20-25 that would moan at me but the banter was good playing on a pitch surrounded by huge trees and sawdust for the lines no shit and the trees behind the top goal they wood be hanging over the goal posts sometimes and needed ripping branches of before one game because there wasn't any money.

Inverurie Juniors 1
Cuminestown 1

INVERURIE JUNIORS— Thomson; Elrick, B D'Arcy, D D'Arcy, Bragg, Whyte, Gunn, Boon, Bruce, Davidson, Wood. Subs — Baxter, Ewens.
CUMINESTOWN — Blagden; Burnett, Bisset, Milne, Morrison, Gillan, Crawford, Murray, Cameron, Steel, Skogh. Subs Scott, McDonald.
Referee — G Middleton, Aberdeen.

CUMINESTOWN opened strongly in this Division 1 encounter and a shot by Cameron looked net bound but D'Arcy did well to block.

A quick break by Wood saw him send over a low cross but Bruce was crowded out by the defence.

Gunn lost the ball in midfield and Steel sent in a fierce shot which Thomson did well to touch over.

Some fine skills by Bruce saw him evade two defenders before sending over a cross which Blagden saved well.

Bruce sent the ball out wide to Wood whose shot was palmed clear by Blagden.

Good battling by Davidson saw him win the ball on the goal line and push it back to Whyte whose effort was deflected inches past.

A good move by the homeside involving four players saw an opening created by Bruce but his final shot went over the bar.

Cuminestown almost opened the scoring when a wind assisted clearance by Blagden forced his opposite number Thomson to touch the ball over the bar.

Minutes from half-time the homeside opened the scoring when a fine crossfield pass by Wood found BRUCE who sent a fierce drive past Blagden from outside the box.

(Half-time: 1-0)

Formartine United 0
Cuminestown 0

FORMARTINE UNITED — Hay, Livingston, Bruce, Mackay, Davidson, Allan, Robertson, Young, Cromar, Rattray, Sutherland. Subs — Jack, Hepburn.
CUMINESTOWN — James; Matthews, Bisset, Milne, J Crawford, Valentine, A Crawford, Murray, Cameron, Jopp, Kerr. Subs — Steele, Trigger.
Referee — G Ross, Aberdeen.

CUMINESTOWN kicked off in perfect conditions and Hay in the home goal had to look lively to cut out a through ball.

At the other end Rattray headed narrowly past the post and Sutherland blasted a good chance over the bar.

Formartine continue to squander chances and the visitors almost took the lead but Hay brought off a great save from Murray.

(Half-time: 0-0)

Formartine United continued on the offensive and a long ball from Rattray found Cromar who cut inside but his shot was turned round the post by keeper James who was in superb form for the visitors.

Cuminestown in a counter attack had a chance but Hay saved well from Cameron.

The home side had an incredible miss late on when both Jack and Rattray had their shots cleared off the line by a fortunate Cuminestown defence.

The visitors almost got the winner in the final minute when Cameron was clean through but he shot the ball over the bar.

Scored the equliser 25 yards out keeper messed up on a muddy winters day so all good.

And as I said help as this was a club in proper free fall without a parachute but give them there due by the time the community was ready to start backing the club again it was far to late was all good I missed playing for the club.

The secretary of the club Andy Bisset RIP gave the Turriff united manager my number who did call me and asked me along to training but as I never drove at the Time and the travel for training. Even though he promised me transport but I choice East End with Andy Milne.

With my two season in junior football from the age of 16-18 I managed a total of 24 goals for the team that came joint bottom in there last year.

So when Andy was given the East End juniors Managers job he made me one of his first sign-ings. At East End juniors I wasn't given a chance to be honest the committee had given Andy the job and there wasn't all of them happy about it and showed it at games and training ses-sions and all that done was create an atmosphere were with all the negativity going on it never helped my confidence at all and I was more than capably at that time to score week in week out especially with John Brown And Allan Douglas on the wings if I was given a run in that team iv no doubt I would of hit double figures.

 But i thought most of the players were pricks and as I say I don't do sub week in week out.

I then moved on as the club at the time had two cracking forwards as iv just mentioned and both had successful careers in the Highland league. There was Micheal Craig loaned out from Aberdeen so my chances were limited as Aberdeen FC paid the junior clubs a fee to play these young players back then or the deal was you got players and you must play them or they wouldn't give that junior club player or players.

Forres Machanics Mosset Park. Capacity 502 seats 2700

I got 20 minutes against Bishopmill United on Forres mechanics pitch done ok East End won 4-0 never scored but showed I could play at that level and other players feared for there places I now see that looking back. And the committee at that time really were at each other and they left the club in a mess. I left due to lack of game time I understood I wasn't going to walk into there side.

Iv came from playing two seasons in the league below to playing for a club that at that time pretended they had big money to win the super league but they sold all there good players after a I left the club so Andy tried getting me back but I had then went and joined Hall Russell United who were in the super league but I had scored and played against them at my Cuminestone days so i knew the manager at the time and I gave it a go to start with as the committee at the time there made me more than welcome as they had watched me rip them apart and scored 2 in my first season in junior football against them so they at the club wanted me there and due to them being in the top league I knew I would have to put in a lot of work to get used to the way they played as a team and I put that effort in and made a few substitute appearances and things were going OK.

I had a other player who stayed close to me so he would pick me and any other players on route to training and games so everything was going ok when I got a few starts scoring one against Sunnybank at home in a 2-1 defeat then without explanation there manager put me back on the bench so he has absolutely no clue about man management and is a nasty piece of work and tells players to go on the park and deliberately hurt the opponent which isn't even a thing I think about before a game so in my mind he is a complete fool and knows nothing about football.

And the short time I was there because as iv said I don't do sub especially when your better than the players he had but they would try making me feel unwelcome and knock my confidence which is really horrible to be sitting in a dressing room that's full of back stabbing players then you tend to lose belief in your own ability.

I used to get so paranoid playing for most junior clubs iv been at due to players fearing for there own places which is something I would never allow in any club I have been in charge of. But after leaving Hall Russell's i joined Parkvale JFC.

They signed me on a pro form so they paid me but I only signed for them due to my old friend Jim Blacklaw who got the managers job and I went up to play Elgin City back then they were a highland league side with players like Ian Poleworth and basically a squad to challenge for the league title. Well after playing a season up front with Jim he pulled me aside because he knew me well and even a friendly being sub pissed me off.

But I understood he wanted to have a look at the new players he had took up for the game thats called man management So after 20 minutes he put me in the middle of the park to try stop this little boy from Kinchorth Ord wll he could play him like but I done my best and we got beat 2-0 with my former school mate Kevin Christie's brother Nicky in goals that day and he kept the score down.

Elgin city Ground Borough Briggs Capacity 478 seats total 4520.

So Jim had a co manager who is a great guy and am not writing lies in this read to keep people happy as you've probably guessed by now but Pat never had been involved in that level of football in his life. Jim on the other hand played at the top level with trials at Leicester City and I knew he wasn't one for talking much but when he did give you any advice you listened due to his experience playing for lower league English football. I learned so much playing up front with him, you can't buy experience but good habits rub off and he should me good habits he loved a pint lol.

Parkvale JFC Ground they are now joined up with Stoneywood JFC and have a new Ground.

Where as Pat had never really played apart from lower league Amateur so you can guess the out come of that relationship as I at the time and still stand by it to this day I knew more about the junior game than him as you've read by the time I had signed for them I was in my 5th season in junior football and was only 21.

Pat gave me my signing on fee after the Elgin Game and I think I played two games and told Pat the truth you don't have a fucking clue now go fuck but since those days Pat is a ok man away from football remember reader this is not a read on me slagging people off am just being honest. Plus all these players they told me they had signed not one of them had and we started the season with a shit team and I felt let down due to me having better offers with other junior clubs Hermes, Lewis United and a few others. But due to my friendship with Jim was the one and only way I went so No more Parkvale.

This is no reflection on Pat as a person away from football as hes helped me out in my football life and normal everyday life and since all that years ago i still class Pat as a good friend who when we started our team he would come watch our games if he had nothing else on plus he worked at the Dug out sports Shop and we would get all our football kits and all other things needed to run a team.

The Torry Battery great walk done it mean times with the kids when they were young

Since were away to speak about Torry so here's the Battery and that was me on a sunday leaping like that dolphin to score again. No but when stayed there I would walk the kids round.

So I was 22 and couldn't play football So aged 22 yrs old I stopped playing junior for 3/4 of a season. So I was staying in Torry and when I was drinking with my ex brother in law I got speaking to the manager of Torry Vics he was looking for player. I told him I had left Parkvale but they had paid me so I couldn't play for any other team due to signing a pro form. Well he looked into things and said I could play.

I played 3/4 of a season for them and ran riot against the teams in that league as I was used to playing against far better players at that time. So I found the net weekly. This story is true we was playing Portlethen and a fight broke out between our keeper and one of there players who had kicked our keeper late when he had the ball. Well he got up and he smacked the so said player in the face and all hell broke loose and they had a old player who started with me and I dropped him with a head butt and due to all the fighting the referee abandoned the game.

And the team got a fine and was allowed to carry on playing in the league so that one memory of playing in the Sunday welfare also remember traveling all the way to Tomintoul in a Scottish cup game pure shambles of a place we got changed in a old horse carriage no shit we had to take turns going in to get changed as it was that small. Picture one of Big John Furys old Travelers vintage horse and chart caravans minus the showers and it was October there was mud sticking to us yet not a drop of water to be seen. But plenty drink and drugs on the trip home think I went home on the Wednesday.

When I was 23 years old I had a shocking injury to my shoulder which after nearly 2 years of messing about in a sling and physio I ended up getting surgery on my right shoulder. Then in that time I ballooned up to 15 stone but after a good preseason I lost 2 stone and joined Dyce juniors and was a sub for the 1st few games getting 15 minutes here and there until for one I really needed to build up my physical but most of all my mental side as I was worried I would be good enough after such a long lay off and was terrified I dislocated my shoulder again as I wouldn't be able to support my family financially because these insurance policies that they had back then were terrible. Not sure how they are nowadays but if you got injured it you got peanuts.

<u>**Muad JFC Football pitch who tried signing me for £500 as Cuminestone were away to fold yet they still refused the cash being offered. I was willing to sign but the club said no.**</u>

<u>**Dyce JFC Football Ground Ian Mair Park.**</u>

<u>**Royals won the treble on that pitch with another Final defeat of poor JBP Thistle**</u>

While playing for Dyce juniors me and Phil helson who iv knew since childhood were both playing in the middle of the park against Lewis united in the semi finals of the Morrison trophy which we won 4-1 and if I remember correctly I was named sponsors man of the match am sure the club could dig that picture out from there archives since I helped them reach there first ever cup final but I was away before the final and Lewis United Finished 2nd that season.

Both of us run the game totally I had been getting a regular start and my fitness was getting higher and in that game i scored and set 2 up one for Phil who was a very good steady player that in my opinion should of played at a higher level as well. This game stands out not just for the fact I had scored but after the game me and Andy plus some of the Dyce players.

We were in a club called full of Balloons as it was known as back then its now Private Eyes on Bridge Street strip club, Well the management team from Lewis united were there to and we all started having a talk about the game when the manager of Lewis united offered me 1k to sign which was ok for junior football 20 years ago but I stayed with the team.

But me being a loyal man I refused the offer even though I was playing on a Amateur form for Dyce juniors I stayed loyal to the club to try and get them promotion out of Division one as I was happy enough playing at Dyce. To me loyalty means a whole lot more in life than money That's one of the main reason I fallout with people due to them having no loyalty at all. So I could of took the grand and left plus would of played ever week. But since Andy had helped me lose weight and get back playing at junior level week in week out after 3 years out. I felt I owed him.

Yet my time with Dyce was going ok I knew the chairman thought I was the worst person to walk earth but every time I played for his team I gave 100% I was getting fitter by the week I just needed to get my confidence back but with me suffering from a mental illness called Cyclothymia I get racing thoughts and impulsive behaviour I can sometimes come across wrong when am the most loyal and honest person you could meet but never mind me for now.

Do you know how hard it is for a person that suffers from that going into a changing room full of people you don't know well it's hard and the last thing you need is someone clearly showing your not wanted and I knew I definitely wasn't part of there long term plans. I remember a OVD Scottish cup game against Whiteletts Victoria Junior club at home so during the week leading up to the game it was competitive training as boys were looking for a start against a team tipped to beat us by Williamhill bookmakers.

I know because I had real issues in the past and still am betting, but I was looking on betting on Dyce winning because we were playing well enough plus most of all we were win games and I was playing games on a weekly basis and was putting my all in at training for a club who wasn't paying me I was going to training twice a week I had a young family and was getting myself back on my feet again after a 3 year lay off due to football.

So anyone who's got young children and a misses nipping your head about what happens if you hurt yourself again, are they going to pay the bills, well the answer to this is no they wouldn't but i loved playing football its all I knew from a young age and in some relationships playing part time football isn't a problem if the club there playing for can cover all there wages and guarantee that in writing theirs not many junior clubs able to do that, so she was right about the injury issues.

Back then when I asked about what sort of cover they had in place I never really got a proper look at there insurance policies enforced on junior clubs and amateur clubs to have some sort of cover in place for players by the SFA.

See things like that people stop people playing when they have family as bills need paying, so I was on an Amateur form playing for nothing sorry got a pair of football boots from the little sports shop in crown street in Aberdeen city center was far more expensive than say JD sports so I needed to put some of my own money towards the copa mundials Adidas for the start of

the season, wasn't the clubs fault looking back they were probably just that used to using that shop for whatever reason. Not sure if its still trading now that you can get most football equipment online from China a lot lot cheaper than him so that's probably not helped his cause any as back in the day his shop sponsored the Junior leagues and cups in the Nort region.

So its Match day versus Whiteletts from Aryshire so am playing there's minutes to go Dyce are winning 3-2 and we got a throw in down the right hand side bottom end of the rabbit hole infested pitch that the chairman spends a good bit of money on the surface but his only chance of having a decent pitch is get a 4g surface as hes not getting rid of the rabbits where the pitch is situated its pure surrounded by rabbits.

So I take my time the referee even had a go at me to hurry up so through the ball to a 18-19yr old David Armour who loses the ball to one of the Whiteletts players and you can guess what happened even though there was another 9 players still on the park behind the ball yet they manage a last kick of the ball eqaliser.

The Whiteletts player that disposed the ball from David ran from one end of the pitch to the other without one player managing to just snap him in bits to stop him not one of the other 8 out field players got anywhere near him and he cooly slotted the ball under were keeper to end the game in a 3-3 draw meaning a replay in Ayr, you should of seen the Chairmens face when we were coming off the pitch was no clapping and smiles that day even though they were odds on at the bookies to beat us the manager is screaming at me a load of bullshit to be brutally honest was as iv just explained there were another 8 out field players that never put a tackle in yet hes standing giving me all this your an experienced player why you rushing a throw in and throwing the ball at a young loon.

All bullshit people it boiled down to the fact he knew me well and totally singled me out in front of a whole dressing room and with me having the issues I suffer daily people hes going nuts at me and the fact we had to pay for buses for the replay saying I had cost the club money and am looking thinking what is going on here are these lot for real never mind we got a draw against a club from Ayrshire which not much North junior clubs did back then especially Dyce Juniors back then, when I joined the club it was on its way up and as I write this Dyce as a club have came along way from there days drawing with Cuminnestone United in which after one game against them they tried signing me as well.

So with me already either being paranoid or spot on the people in the background never gave me a chance, I was coming back from a long lay off and needed time as when I was getting frustrated with team mates not being up to that standard of football both fitness wise and ability some were there only because they were either liked by the board or were mates with a decent player.

But I understand you cant have a squad of good players when your not paying them and some of the players weren't good enough to play junior football fact, so I made my feelings clear, the players who were not getting any grief were on the same park as I was playing that day I remember I went home deflated after that game and thought about giving it up as I was feeling totally dejected I had knew Andy and had played for him since aged 16 and am 10 years older and hes spoke to me like it was my fault.

I wasn't captain or anything like that but along with the chairman's look after the game in my head they never wanted me there, and I was a good signing for free back then as I had other options but When Andy phoned me asking if I wanted to come along I really thought he would try give me time but the club was going through player like you wouldn't believe but I was there with loads of junior experience and boys straight out of under 18s trying to tell me about junior football, but they fitted the Narrative the chairman wanted to go with and still does to this day, never wanted a player like me who would roll my sleeves up and get stuck in and try to enforce myself in the middle of the park chopping a few people down when need be but just sit as a holding midfield player till I got fitter and more mobile.

I never need told how to play the game as I knew unlike these young headless chickens running about doing nothing but losing the team games at times just like this game against Whiteletts all it need that game was a player with the intelligence to take a card red if be then no buses needed, but the chairman who pulls all the strings there along with a few of his friends wont have players that will think like that and shout and swear at team mates which as you see worked for me and my own team and ever team needs as I call an enforcer in the center of the park that can pass a ball fact.

Whiteletts junior football team Scottish cup replay so I was popular at training as boys like Phil Helson was taken the piss haha were all getting a bus trip and its all your fault as Phil knows the game so he even thought along with Steven Webster I got it bad from Andy after the game which we all thought at the time was unjust considering these younger fools couldn't play at all and the ones that could play there heads were up there own arse.

Iv been in the Dyce JFC changing room and had a player who was at that club at the time who soon left and moved on to Elgin telling me being completely serious, remember were playing in the first division of the North junior league and iv a team mate after me, still coming down from the weekend that he and his agent were trying to get him a trial at Aberdeen I thought I was tripping people.

He really in his own head believed he was good enough to play senior level which he did but not with Aberdeen mad man. Hes one of the most self centered persons iv played the game with he wouldn't pass the ball ever as if I or any other player scored and he never he would sulk like a child honest people you really haven't met such a greedy fucker on the pitch, of the pitch I never socialized with him or most of the other players as to be honest a lot were studying and becoming police officers like my former team mate Mr Richie Mcrae so I definitely wasn't up for socilsing with them.

As I say were getting game time here and there, So we traveled south for the replay but players that couldn't be fucked traveling with the team to Ayr as they really never put in 100 percent some of them not all.

So game starts there's a dog track round there pitch which was boggy due to the great Scottish October weather was a flat big surface but cut up as the game got under way totally different conditions to the one when the clubs first met ending in us being in the middle of a dog track getting kicked stupid from Whiteletts who's players knew the referee just like up here its all the same referees if your playing week in week out you get to know them especially if your the type of player I was always been spoken to but nothing malice as iv only a few times playing have I ever wanted to break someones leg.

Was Sunnybank JFC former player who played center of defence my memory fades me what his name was but he pure wiped me out when I was just young think I was in my first season at Cuminestone United we played them at Heathryfold Park he was playing at the back and I nut megged him and laughed calling him an old cunt and he said to me do that again and am going to put you up in the air well I laughed went searched for the ball and the next time I was running at pace at him and done it again, well he wasn't lying he said think your funny even though we were getting beat 4-5 nil he got all excited with himself and nearly broke my leg I was in agony but stayed on for a bit but just could shack it off big animal think the end result was 8-0, if he hadn't put me in bits I would of scored that day as I normally got one against the bigger teams I used to try to impress sometimes I did then other games I would try to hard rather than just playing my game, but I hated join a new club as I would again question my own ability, and start sweating and feeling proper anxious yes me people used to have panic attacks nearly and would pace the floor in my house hours before games, mad folks but the game in Ayr never went our way but I just took it as another step towards getting back totally fit so the 4-1 defeat wasn't unexpected as at home getting such a great result then a excuse for the team to get a piss up on the way home.

In my mind that's the good times to play as your not playing the same teams plus it is all part of team bonding well on this bus trip home I sat at the back of the bus out pissed off we got beat and this lot are happy we got beat 4-1 only a few players were even drinking worst Scottish cup bus trip iv been on, when we got back into Aberdeen most of the players went home well me Phil and a few others plus manager Andy was there.

So we went for a few drinks and out of the whole squad I think there was maybe 5 of us so great team bonding and I was a father of two girls and I still stayed out for a few drinks even though I knew I would get grief from kids mum. Yet these players wouldn't even come for a drink with the manager as iv said great team. I was becoming fitter with games and I wasn't being paid unlike most of the other players for playing and going to training after work and sometimes not seeing your children till late so playing junior football there's a lot more than just ability at that level required but never play for free in junior football if there's even one player getting paid I that team which they try and hide due to the unrest it would cause in the dressing room .

But as I say I gave 100% until one game against Turriff United who had a great midfield and I had been playing well sitting in the middle of the park braking play up and putting in a shift and tacking and that's a art by the way being able to do a simple thing like tackle. Well as I was saying I was playing weekly and that week I was at training as usual and there was one of the players that in my eyes wasn't anywhere near able to play junior football but this is the game that broke the camels back. The boy he picked to play in the middle of the park Ray sorry mate your not a junior player and that's me being nice. Andy only picked him due to the fact he was friends with half the team.

So we're playing Turriff united at Ian Mair and am hungover to fuck if I remember I was on it all night and now am in the centre of the pitch chasing the fittest two midfield players in the league with this useless player. That on the Thursday night training he took an asthma attack and needed help in Torry Academy where the training was true story folks this man couldn't breathe on the Thursday yet on the Saturday he's playing in the center of the park pure madness. Even if I wasn't hungover I couldn't have carried him. But believe this or not they hit the bar 5-6 times in the first half and we were 2-0 up.

So coming up for halftime I felt sick because of the night before plus carrying him I was looking on get off but they wouldn't take me off so I was sick all over the sideline which I never wanted to do if I was subbed then I could of made the toilet and never made a mess on the side line. After that I just walked off and got booked by the referee for leaving the pitch without his permission. That was the last thing on my mind I was totally embarrassed by it and ended up arguing with Andy Milne the Dyce JFC manager and throw the tie at him and grabbed a beer from the fridge in the players lounge bit and that was the end of me with Dyce JFC and junior football for good at 26-27 years of age and I helped Dyce win the Morrison Trophy in the season of 2001/02 and had I stayed I would have had a winners medal.

So after leaving Dyce JFC I said to my younger brother Scott who by the way had also been playing junior football but had lost interest along with a few boys I knew myself that were good players but needed to start playing again so we tried starting a team and we ended up called Royals bar FC at the beginning we had 10 players and a liter and a half of Evian water training at the Aberdeen Lads club pitches out of the 10 at least 7 had played highland league youth teams or been warming a bench somewhere in the juniors. One of the players John Barry is mother's friend worked in a pub called the Royals so one thing lead to another and the pub agreed to sponsor the team as long as the players went back for a beverage after the games he also used to lay out sandwiches but eat with a warning.

So we joined the Sunday welfare league after me and my middle brother Andrew went to the league entry meeting and paid the fees and we were in division 2 as the Royals we had worked hard to get a full Squad and strips training equipment and basically we had everything in place for our First ever proper game as a team, we had some steady players for that level but we were blessed with other players who were all disillusioned by the game due to one reason or another, so we had a squad of eighteen players which gave me a problem for our first game of the season as if you aren't familiar with football you can only pick sixteen player for a game so that meant two of the boys who had joined at the start of the team, so that wasn't nice to tell two of them they weren't even getting a kit but both understood.

The first Royals Team and first game .

But that's one of the reasons I would go mad at players at times because I was putting my all into the team like going on a Sunday morning to league meetings at 10am on a Sunday morning and if no one from the club was there to represent the club then you would be fined so money was tight enough as it was without being fined for silly things like not going to a 1 hour meeting depending on what kind of mood I was in then it would go on all day.

As people who run lower league teams will know money and sponsorship is hard to come by at the best of times, its a good team of people round you if your going to be successful at all things in life it takes a good team of people. So its game time for the Royals iv been running the game through my head who to pick and to be honest the team picked itself but I was a total bag of nerves leading up to our first competitive game but I had faith in the squad.

So I picked the team the both player who were disappointed but were men about it due to the fact I had properly thought out why I was leaving both out of the squad I gave them valid reasons which were true so the boys understood and probably if more managers even in work were honest and give you a valid reason then people have more respect for you.

Teams picked and out comes the new white Nike kit and I bought black and white socks with the kit so when in winter try getting white socks clean in the winter months, so game starts nerves gone and we won 6-3 so we were 5-0 up at one point but we got the three points and so that first season we went on a sixteen league game unbeaten run before losing to that seasons rivals JBP Thistle 3-1 in a midweek game which are a nightmare but going all that time unbeaten in the league was a great achievement for a team just put together in the summer of that season so in total we lost two games all season drew four and scored 157 goals lost 44 and collected 70 points in 28 games.

That's 5.6 goals a game which is a crazy total to have at any level especially for a teams first season. So our first season we won the league and both league cups.

In one of our games in the welfare as the Royals and we were playing a league game against rivals JBP Thistle when I Was sent of for 2 yellows the team were one nil down there's minutes to go d we got a corner and my brother Scott went into there box and the corners been played into the penalty area were the balls bouncing about and it lands straight onto my brothers right foot and the ball went crashing into the net.

My idea was what is the difference if we get beat 2-0 or grab an incredible equaliser which was the case in this game. The whole team and support went crazy your 1-0 down with seconds to go and your goalie equalizes and grabs the team a great point. We also won the Eric turner trophy on Dyce Juniors pitch Ian Mair park beating JBP Thistle 1-0 in a windy day with Craig Murrison grabbing the winning goal. As the royals we won the John kilminster trophy at Culter Juniors pitch Crombie park beating arch rivals JBP Thistle 6-1 in a great team performance.

Second season the team lost the league in the final kick of the ball in a league game with ropes and lines men never seen before in the welfare league got cheated fact. Plus that season a couple of the players had a flat with lap dancers staying with them so I blame them for us losing the league due to all the players back at the flat partying.

During my run as player manager with the Royals Fc I gave all these players doing a job that they could do and didn't expect as much success as we had in the two great season In welfare league winning the league and both cups in the same season when at the beginning we started with nothing as I said. But due to the lap Dancers using the local sex shop the owner bought the team a Nike kit which was nice of him so nice new white kit for the team to run onto the pitch looking the part but could we all play as a team as we only had two friendly games before we started the season but we had a great pre season so every player knew there jobs.

Also Runners up in a league decider midweek game with me having a fucked right knee was my medial collateral ligament got done in a quarter final Scottish cup game against a team from Elgin it was that bad I had to leave the pitch and iv never done that. So I played 1/4 of the season out my nut on my fathers solpadol all we needed was a draw and we got a goal I scored chopped off when Davie Armour actually cut the ball back from the byline so it was a simple tap in yet the linesman for a league game remember chopped it off and you can't be offside if the ball is cut back so that was a goal we got cheated out of. Then we got a penalty and Both Craig Murison and David Armour with over a 100 goals between them knew my knee was Fucked and am looking at them and they both bottled it.

So I took the pen decent pen but keeper saved it. There sideline was packed ours had a few no one wanted us to win that day so they went one nile up and I was getting it sticking from there sideline which just spurred my on more and with 8 minutes to go I scored a cracker and ran along there sideline giving them it sticking.

So remember they cloverleaf hadn't beaten us all season in 4 games played previously beating them 4-1, 3-1, 4-1 in the league and beat them in the semi finals of both the Joe Paterson trophy and the Cruickshank cup 2-1 that season so with minutes to go I had the ball in there corner and Lewis smith decided to cross the ball into there box. We had not one player in

there box so there 6ft-6" goalie caught the ball then kicked it into our box and my brother pulled of a great save and turned the ball round the post at the bottom right of the goal for a corner.

So iv asked the referee how long to go he replied after this corner so iv told Lewis who has caused all this by crossing the ball into the hands of a giant goalie instead of kicking it out for a throw or just help it up game over league winners. But no with time up we have to defend a corner. So I've told Lewis to pick there player up and his brother and captain to do the same and the both got it wrong and the boy I told them to pick up scored a easy header from 6 yards out game over runners up but we were really the best team in the league.

The Royals FC start of season 2003/04

We also got to a few finals and we never turned up and we had injuries and suspensions and boys working ie my brother the keeper. Now everyone knows that runs a football team need a good keeper or we wouldn't have got to finals as he was a junior standard goalie playing in the welfare which was a big asset to the team. So he was working my striker Craig Morrison who was a goal a game ratio so another big miss. So we played Shirlaws with a depleted team also missing myself in the final of the Joe Patterson Memorial trophy losing 3-2 at Parkvale juniors pitch.

Then we played them again in the trophies international cup final in season 2004-05 the were defiantly our bogie team only beating them three times in the league twice 3-0 and then 3-2 but they inflicted our heaviest defeat in the clubs history I thought I would make big changes and that day I gave other players a chance and it back fired badly with a 6-1 league but out of the league format of 10 teams in the division playing each other 4 times we beat both Shirlaws and Cloverleaf 3 times.

But we clicked as we normally did with a full squad and it was against JBP Thistle and there wasnt one player had a bad game and it was some team performance that day and we beat them 4-0 and won the Cruickshank cup with me getting two that day.

We also played Shirlaws in another final again with a depleted squad again with myself and a few other players that were very important players to the team. We lost to them again in the George Scott Trophy at Hall Russell's ground 3-2.

There was a semi final cup game against a team run by some former players and supporters of a former power house of welfare football back when I was smashing them in at junior level they won most trophy's including the Scottish cup. So there was a bit of niggle but nothing much than to say other than Davie Armour ripped them to bits, as me and Craig Murison were both suspended so we won easy 4-0.

But as iv said in our second season the fact two of our players had lap dancers from London staying in there flat so all the players were partying in there every Saturday night. Hadn't that happened plus we lost David Armour who went go Cove amateurs which never worked out and he returned but we were doing well enough without him but a player who scored 70 goals the previos season try replacing that so with all that factors we worked through but had he been in the squad from the start we most definitely would of took every trophy that we lost in but still a great effort for a team only two seasons old.

Me when I had hair leaping like a Salmon.

There was one midweek game when we were struggling with work injuries suspensions. Anyone running a football team at any level it's a nightmare end of season games. So like every other teams we used the fact you could use to trialist so I had phoned loads of players when I was driving along Blanagask road in Torry and seen my young mate Andrew Ewen walking along the road. Next thing he knew he was in a sports shop picking a new set of boots to play for the Royals and he scored 2 in a 5-1 win so that's the joys of lower league football.

Here's another story not football involved but since we're speaking about Andrew Ewen now player Manger of Kinchorth Amateurs well I was working on the galaxy 3 oil rig that's a Jack up drilling rig. That was stuck to the buzzard platform well I was part of the helideck crew and one time i opened the chopper doors and here's Andy Ewen with a big cheese grin on his face that was his first ever trip offshore and he meets me on the helideck soon as the doors open.

That was years ago now think he's still on that platform.
Anyone running a football team in the lower leagues knows leagues are won and lost in the Northeast is in the summer mid week games.

as it's not easy running an Amateur team as boys have to work injuries suspensions it's hard work running any team so if you play football and your reading this remember the effort the people running the show are putting in for you not to sell 5 sweepers fact of running football teams.

We had the best of training for being a Sunday league team which wasn't cheap in Aberdeen take Strikers For 55 minutes And Goals is not cheap especially if you book the big pitch but we sold enough sweepers well my uncle Donald sold at least 50 a week but most weeks he would sell 80-120 that help plus one of his work collages won the jackpot a week after new year and it was £3k odds and he never even bought the club a training ball greedy fucker.

There's only ever been one carry on when we were playing in the Sunday league in two seasons and it was with JBP Thistle who were our main rivals in division 2 coming runners up in both league cups and runners up in the league.

We played them in a mid week fixture at Hazelhead pitches full squad well as best I was getting with 6.30pm Kick offs and all threat that goes along with running non league team. So were running a mock and there midfield player lost it and threatened to beat me up after the game well I took that as a threat and after the game in which we won 4-0 he came walking out towards me so I smacked him and put him out cold and as he was going to the ground his kit bag saved his head as he landed on his bag perfectly.

So a few of his team mates started so the got chased for there life's true story I was kicking them about the car park mad. So 4 match ban and the club had to write a letter of apology which was done in a nice and correct way even though I never started the situation.

So after seasons two ended we had played 49 won 33 drew 4 lost 12 scoring 189 goals and conceding 105 so in two seasons we played 92 yes 92 games in two seasons and in 2003 the Scottish weather was terrible and just rained and games were off every week for a few months so we had a real build up of games and the players were burned out playing Sunday Tuesday Thursday Sunday on hard pitches and we done that for weeks on end.

The players were picking up little injuries here and there and to the lead up to the league decider we were totally burned out and the Cloverleaf team had 2 weeks rest before playing us which will have helped them no end and why the game was played on a Thursday night rather than playing it on the Sunday as it was for the league title and would of gave my team a few days rest but we tried and came up short, in that 92 games we won 65 drew 8 and lost 19 scoring 394 losing 174 goals so that's an average of nearly 4.3 goals a game and conceding nearly 1.9 goals a game. So after two seasons in Sunday league Craig got 110 goals and went AWOL a good few games in season two David 118 so that's a great pairing and I was lucky enough to have both and every other quality players the club has had.

All these premiership Managers are playing a 4-3-3 System I like to play a 4-2-4 when going forward as I would always have pace on the flanks that can have the fitness and ability to get a cross in the box which is vital if your playing with 2 wide men but they must be able to play box to box as when you lose the ball your midfield turns into a 4-5-1 as you get one of the front two to drop back so you've a 5 in the midfield.

But you need players with the ability they can be as fast as Usain Bolt but if they cant tackle or get a cross when they get to the oppositions box then there no good so here's some tips I practiced for hours was stick Skinny in goals when he got old enough to play and just spend time crossing the ball and free kicks and just getting more confident as what I practiced became habit in games being comfortable on the the ball and also would kick the ball against a wall night and day, I basically carried a ball with me and would go in early at Primary school just to play football before class with friends from the school team like Jim Christie Jr who's father was president of the Sunnbank Club as club committee as hes dedicated a lot of his life to helping the Junior club, well Jim Jr was one player that would be there before the bell went jackets for goal posts Jim himself played upfront for a few junior sides as well over the years and am still friends with him to this day even though I always ask him if he has a medal from Middlefield Primary school sorry Jim.

Not a bad return for a team 2 seasons

So after two season playing Sunday football we moved into the Aberdeenshire Amateur football league after having to stand in Pittodrie stadium in front of a large number of other club members. And people who know me would of thought I took it all in my stride well I did but due to the mental illness I suffer from Cyclothymia I get racing thoughts and my brain gets over loaded and get myself all in a panic and I always manage to get through these difficult situations but I must admit it's a bit donning.

So I managed to get through it with my two friends lee Cheeser and David Longmuir who was a great man and help to the success of the club with managing to get the boys everything they ask for Dave would get a sponsor as he was a buyer for an Aberdeen oil company. Believe me so for a brand new club that's only 2 years old to have Nike kits tracksuits bags training gear boots and petrol money for away games. And the biggest draw of all a junior pitch to play on. And we got our fair share of games on that pitch for the cost of £25 a game. We were wearing Nike kits since season 2002-3 on wards as we had great sponsors.

So we changed the team name from Royals to East End Amateurs as we joined up with the club and we sold sweepers weekly and the deal was we paid £25 towards the prize and used the other money for winter training mostly at goals in the summer nights it's a lot cheaper to run a team properly because it's very costly for training facilities across Aberdeenshire.

So our first season in the Amateurs kicked off the new season with hopes of promotion but we didn't have a great start I was the trying to replace a pairing upfront that had scored over 126 goals between them in a very short space of time we lost 2 out of our first 5 games then Craig Murison returned and first game with a decent squad we beat Westdyke 4-1 with Me getting 2 and Craiger getting 2 so we then went 10 unbeaten as iv said David Armour who wasn't even playing football till I gave them all a chance, at the time its frustrating when you lose good players. But I take pride in the fact he was playing every week for Stoneywood in the super league still hitting the net on a regular basis so players like that are hard to replace in the lower leagues believe me.

We were wearing Nike kits every season in the Amateurs as we had to have matching kits with all the other affiliated teams plus simple thing like a nice kit can get you 9-12 a season so the Nike kits in my opinion are the most comfortable and light when it pisses of rain which is most weeks in Aberdeen.

<u>East End Amateurs with a 9-1 win and me slotting a penalty away easy</u>

ON THE SPOT: Steve Cameron sends the Portlethen goalie the wrong way to score a penalty for East

Floodgates oper
second half for

East End Ams 9
Portlethen Utd ...1

We played Bervie AFC down there I was injured and my middle brother was playing but before the game he was speaking to the referee before the game and he's showing my brother his new eBay red and yellow cards he bought saying I can't wait to use them well the game was tight when my brother bent down on our side to take the throw in we were awarded when the bervie player kneed my brother in the ribs and he throw the ball off the bervie players face and knew he was getting a red so was walking off the football pitch when the referee kept shouting on him to come back.

Well he returned to face the referee to give him the red card. My brother was ragging and grabbed his new eBay cards he couldn't wait to show got ripped to bits. He received a 6 months ban and the club was fined £150 which he paid but was funny. Plus he stayed just up the road from Bervie in Montrose so knew the players by there first names. So that was the beginning of the end in my opinion.

One game we was playing Portlethen out there and my kids mums brother played for my team for a few seasons now he's mixed race so the young boys drinking on Portlethens sideline started calling him Luther van Ross which was funny due to the fact they were taking the piss because we were beating them so you expect a bit of banter between players and other teams sideline even your own team mates will give you stick but I put a stop to it and the game finished without any harm done to anyone apart from Potlethens chances of getting promoted.

But there's a situation where really our players getting racially abused in some people's eyes and if they had handled the situation in a different manner then all hell could of let loose as I wouldn't have stood for any player playing for my team to be bullied in anyway fact.
But had we East end had made a fuss nothing would have been done by that Amateur committee back then

So back to the first season in Aberdeenshire Amateur league we came 4th after a really bad start. To anyone reading this that thinks running any sort of football team isn't easy and to run and also be successful isn't an easy job Believe me so for a brand new club that's only 2 years old to have Nike kits tracksuits bags training gear boots and petrol money for away games.

Is not a bad feat and if your reading this and iv played against you through the years there is no way I never entertained people with my madness and skills at times but I was fair until your team started kicking players up in the air then you knew I was coming for you at some point of the game or better still I would score and just smile worse than any bad challenge than losing a goal fact.

During our first season we done a lot better than I thought remember the Welfare league was at hazelhead every week unless you had a Scottish cup tie when we had these ties we would play them on a junior pitch if I could get one which normally wasn't a problem due to games being a Sunday, now were in a league where your playing all over Aberdeenshire and some players don't drive or don't have transport or they don't want to put miles on there cars.

So you have the added pressure of getting a team to say Stonehaven 6.30pm kick off before any bypass was built so you can imagine how hard it is for Amateur clubs are under especially when your hated by jealousy plus the fact people wanted to see me fail but the more people think I cant do something the more I want to prove that I will have the last laugh, look at the side I had then Lost too many players at the start of the season lost my both strikers one came back the other as I said moved into the North junior super league, Ryan Cooper ex Rothes Youth player and ever present for 2 seasons stopped playing due to work, Lewis Smith was away on it for most of the second and third season after being named Players player of the year which shows he was a great player him and David Armour both natural left footed plus Steven Batty so we were blessed on the left side of the team and they used to tear teams apart.

So try replacing players like them at the level we were playing at you cant I tried even though Steven and Lewis did play a good few games in the Amateurs and made a big difference to the team but as the stats show in games that when we did get beat they could of went our way had we had a consistent team week in week out like we previously had on a Sunday.

But one game in our first season in the amateurs we played a game winning 7-1 on the 11-12-04 with this being the first time in all my years playing football we had a women referee Norma Watt taking charge of probably her 10th game or something she had a great career being fast tracked to the top by the SFA.

Who at that time was making it look like they were away to flood senior football with women referees yet as I write this it took them till September 2017 where Lorraine Watson was the very first women to referee a Scottish men's senior game being Edinburgh City vs Berwick Rangers Watson from a small Fife town called Thornton who also have a junior side call Hibs JFC so its 16 years plus on and still no women has refereed a Scottish Premier league game. See these committees on the SFA they will never allow a women to referee a top flight game but must be seen to be going with the Narrative of that era where shit loads of cash got pumped into advertising and it could of went to grass roots football for both sexes and that would of made more of a difference than pretending that one day a little girl who's dreamed about referring an old firm cup final or league decider cant wait for the SFA to allow one of there qualified women referees to take charge of that type of game and prove that women really have a chance of referring these big games.

So during season one speaking about referees I only got 5 yellow cards the whole of the first season in Amateur football so hardly a thug plus I scored 18 goals from the center of the park is a good return especially since my right knee was still giving me jib I played the whole season though and as iv just said 5 yellow cards.

So season one ended with as iv said with a game at new Advocates in which I took no part in anything to do with East End Amateurs that day even though the word of one man got me banned and as iv said he was treasurer of the league After the game I went in to use the toilet facilities as I wanted a piss the slimly fucker said I was basically running the team it was the last game of season one of our Amateur Adventure we were in 4th spot was secured win or loss and on my kids life's.

The players and the management team put all the players names in a hat and I got a 2 year ban for taking a halftime team talk was having a Laugh with the boys as players were playing all in different positions too there normal position my brother scored a hatrick the game ended 5-2 and I was only serving a 2 game ban for yellow cards but due to me being manager I got 2yrs people is that fair in amateur football. according to the treasurer who was at one of East End Amateurs game pretending to be doing a team story stuck me in for going into the changing rooms for a piss.

And these appeal committees that the seniors go in front of so you would think they would see ense but no there thick as fuck no wonder players wont play amateur football. This was the ast game of season 2005 and then the club were sent a letter from the AAFA then I got one.

All this happened at new Advocates park which at the time the nearest toilet was in the chang- ng rooms as there was also a public one which I went in to use. I would give the changing rooms a sweep as well just like the other teams using the dressing rooms as a social club mem- er I had the key for all parts of the changing rooms as when we were at home the deal for the use of there facilities was I would make sure everything was off and locked up due to the Ju- iors Committee and other club officials would be at there match.

After the game I went in to use the toilet facilities as I wanted a piss as iv said the sneaky fuck- r said I was basically running the team it was the last game of season one of our Amateur Ad- venture we were in 4th spot was secured win or loss and on my kids life the players and the management team put all the players names in a hat and I got a 2 year ban for taking a half ime team talk was having a Laugh with the boys as players were playing all in different posi- ions to there normal position my brother scored a hatrick the game ended 5-2.

Why would he turn up at our meaningless last game of the season where there was plenty peo- le all gathered along East End fenced off from the pitch area chatting as it was a fine Scottish ummers day my children and ex partner were also at the game watching either there family riends or partners and I never even watch hardly any of that game as I was in the club hav- ng a pint checking my football coupon. So as iv went over he and he alone managed to get me a 2yr ban to kick off season two.

One Game we were playing Byron STS in a league game at shedsocksley sports fields the ref- eree was our great friend from the Bervie Caley game where my middle brother tore up his brand new cards from ebay up infront of his face the referee in question caused our club so much trouble was unreal he stayed in Montrose yet he only got £28 for refereeing the game so why he was made to travel all the way to Aberdeen.

I wonder why the league Secretary appoint him why because he had it in for us but anyway the game gets under way and within 10 minutes were dowe to 10 men red card for one of our defenders for at most a booking even the Byron team were astonished at the red card so the game gets back going and Byron STS had a big ginger lad playing and he was basically trying to snap players legs and the ref wasn't interested in our appeals for him to get him told. So one of our players Paul's friend was on our sideline watching the game when one of the Byron players started arguing with the boy watching so iv told the Byron player to calm down so the game ends and were all happy after even playing 80 minutes with 10 men we over came that and beat them 5-2.

So were all on our way to the changing rooms and the ginger big lad from the Byron slapped me hard round the head in front of the ref so am ragging mad plus there other player is giving it large to Paul's friend so I told him to come in with our team changing room as he was wor- ried they tried all hitting him, now on my kids life I knew nothing what this was all about so some of our players got changed and were leaving the dressing room and I told them all to stay just in case it kicked off outside so we have left and iv came to the front of the sports cen- ter and had my own wet kit bag and the whole entire team kit over another shoulder and these two who were arguing are in the middle of the front doors of the center car park rolling about and the big ginger lad is standing over the pair so iv said to him stand back and leave them to sort it out fairly even though it wasn't the place or time but it was happening and others who were using the other facilities in the center are walking past honest mad then next thing the ginger big lad has called our mixed race player a Nigger and I said what did you just say as the mixed race player is my kids uncle so it pissed me off well hes cracked me a free one and buzzed me up a bit so I dropped both bags quick smart and gave him it and he started running round the cars so after just playing 90 minutes I couldn't be fucked chasing the fanny who got 2 smacks back and ran.

So next thing both clubs were pulled up in front of the disciplinary committee where the secretary of Byron was a real stand up guy and told the truth and I still got banned even though the referee never put a report in as he never seen the whole situation the chairmen of the amateurs laughed and said Stevie we will give u the benefit of the doubt what fucking doubt am thinking the mans just told you morons what happened had I been a GRASS the big ginger lad would have been charged with assault yet iv not said nothing to anyone and hes smiling telling me hes giving me the benefit of the doubt and banned me for 56 days and fined me I was in amazement I could believe my ears.

So our stats for season 2004/05 so we played 28 league games wining 17 drawing 2 and 9 losses as I said we lost stupid goals which in turn makes it hard to win games and the strikers I tried weren't as good its as simple as that as the club was moving in the direction all these players asked for and maybe me saying the players I tried really weren't good enough must sound brutal but the partnership Lewis Smith on the left side of midfield went AWOL at the beginning of that 1st season and on his day he was a great player, Then lost my top scorer David Armour who was getting paid and told me he would stay if I paid him £1500 a season in the amateurs apart from its illegal I couldn't pay him unlike other amateur clubs do.

Then not Craig, Lewis, my brother Captain and ever present Chris smith and Redmond Smith Allan Reid who was another ever present and Dean Davidson would all want paying so that was a no no plus he was going to be playing in a higher level thanks to me getting him back playing and finding his confidence again he moved on to bigger and better things. In our first amateur season we still had 9 players that were with the club from day one out of the squad of 18 but we lost top players in key positions.

I like to attack a good keeper and a striker that's greedy but scores goals from nothing are hard to find in amateur football but for all the new experiences that I and the club committee had to deal with we done really we considering all these obstacles that we came up against.

Hampden Scotland's home Ground

Well Players of the year was Chris Smith AKA Muff Player, Player of the Year Scott Cameron AKA Skinny, Top Goal Scorer was Ian Flett with 29 goals Ian was given to the team from the Junior team manager and committee to give him games. Which we did and he got on really well scoring all them Goals in as many games as he joined a good few games into the season.

Most improved and ever present Ian Henderson who a few junior clubs were sniffing about as he was fit as you could be well for a part time amateur player who never drank hardly and done what was asked of him and that was get stuck in and win the ball and pass it to one of our more skillful players and he done that perfect the reason me Lee and Davie all agreed on him without a shadow of a doubt he deserved that.

Young Player of the year was Grieg Mcsloy AKA Homer he was fit and got stuck in and listen to what he was being instructed to do as he was playing weekly was experienced players who would help him at times, This trophy maybe to the players it means nothing but Club man of the year was my uncle Donald Robertson who sold sweepers every week that allowed the club to hire winter training facilities with the amount he would sell so he was a great person to have in the background that some players never probably appreciated how much support financially we got from his efforts every week and it would drive me crazy when players couldn't even sell 5 sweepers yet hes selling shit loads at his work Total.

He got presented with a crystal decanter with engraved silver plate with his name on along with a silver decanter dish for it engraved as well with a personal message which he still has so we thought that would be a nice touch we also gave Assistant Manager Lee Cheesers son Jordan who was only 9 years old and would attend most if not all our matches as his father would take him along he was given support of the year at the clubs end of season trophy night held at the Clubs social clubs events area which had a great turn out from most players and there friends and wives partners.

We held some money raising events on the night and raised more money for the start of season two as you need to pay a good bit of money at the start like league fees and alike. So we played a total of 28 league games the wins draws and loses you've read but we scored 96 goals and conceded 55 Goals so as you can see where our problem was tight games where even though we scored nearly 100 goals in 28 games if we still had the quality of even a few of them game changer players the club had.

As I like to attack as the stats don't lie we scored 96 and coincided 55 so that's 3.4 goals a game but losing 1.9 goals a game so out of the 9 defeats that's games that could quite easy ended up wins but as they say its a funny old game.

I don't worry about how good the other team are worry about how good your own team is and that all the players understand what there jobs are and tell them what there good at and your half way there to a stuffy side which we were looking at some of the teams we lost to we would of beat easy if we had not had silly midweek games miles away at stupid kick off times as iv said unless there's a team running away with the league then its won or lost in the stack of games in midweek fact especially if your one of the teams challenging for honors its hard going believe me. So that was our first season in the AAFA.

We did have a friendly game with Dyce Juniors in season 2004/05.

Our game had been called off due to the pitches being water logged the usual in Aberdeen, Some of the council pitches are a total disgrace and the SNP government need to start spending more money on upgrading the facilities there providing for the price they charge. We as iv just said had no game and Andy called as Dyce juniors game with Dufftown was also called off. But Ian Mair park pitch of Dyce juniors was playable.

I told our players that the game was on and it was at Dyce pitch because they used to let us use there facilities often due to my friendship with there club plus I was a former player. him. So I had a full squad basically and Dyce Juniors had the squad they would of took to Dufftown.

So Andy managed to get a referee and I had conned the players into thinking we had a league match because if I hadn't my number one striker would of fucked it off and went AWOL,

I picked the team minus Mr Armour who had moved on as iv said but by this time I had a settled front two of Dean Davidson and Ian Flett who was lightening fast just his confidence on the ball wasn't there when he first came along from the Juniors but we still had plenty of good players In our squad the problem at times was not having them all at once, But the pair upfront were scoring goals and the team was by the time we played them that day full of confidence so I played myself in the center of the park as that's were at 28 years old and having got back fit and healthy I was more effective there as I could organise the shape of the team.

Plus I was losing my pace so I had a pairing upfront who both knew where the net was most times Dean Davidson who played upfront for most of the season with Ian Flett scored 47 goals Between them in our first season and Craig Murison getting 6 after playing as many games all season plus me grabbing 18 from center midfield wasn't a bad return.

Lewis Smith got 9 from the left side of midfield plus we had a reserve goalkeeper Alex and in games against teams that weren't as good I would play my youngest brother who could score a goal back then as he was fit and he hit the net 9 times so it was handy because if we had players missing I would assess what players we had available and he was always an option upfront and use Alex who was at every game as he would help out with lots of various tasks I would give him and he was dependable person to have a round the club.

So we were an attacking side as my way at looking at football is that if you have goals pace all over the wide positions in the middle one sits one runs and the pair upfront are hitting the net your laughing and If you have a good goalkeeper central defender even better. You can carry a few players if the spine of your team is solid. Myself scoring a peach with that Nike real premiership balls each costing £70 and we had half a dozen.

Yet one or two amateur referees really made us play without them as he wouldn't know a real ball as it was staring him in the face. Good enough for the premiership but not the Aberdeen amateurs, So that game against Dyce Juniors we beat them 2-1.

But in the amateurs you can carry a few players but in the Junior Game you can't carry anyone and should have a full squad all fighting for places. Especially if your spending money but that doesn't always bring success.

Well game starts they get an early goal then we equalise in the second half then with 10 minutes to go iv hit the Nike total 90 Aerow English premiership balls at the time straight into the top corner from the halfway line and you would have stopped it with two goalkeepers. See the delight I got for the team to have beaten the eventual 1st Division league just showed the quad I had when everyone was fit and available as it's not easy running an Amateur team as boys have to work and things always pop up. But that was one of the more memorable games to get one over on my old club.

There was a game at Inverdee and the player smashed the Nike ball into the river Dee and I made him after the game go in chest deep to get the ball. Boy was a clown doing a peter Kay have it on the pitches right next to the river not losing a expensive ball because again His team were being hammered and he decided to do that well bet he never forgets that game fool.

AND mentioning Hammerings.

So I took preseason training got a decent side most players had been at the club from day one like Christopher Smith Steven Batty and Dean Davidson Alan Reid, and I get a letter telling me iv to go to a disciplinary meeting So I ended up with a great start to 2006 season a 2 year ban so that broke my heart I was 30 and got banned for the treasurers allegations his word against mine it must of been heart breaking for the long term players not only me. And I left the club I built from scratch along with others help to the hands of the boys that were running things and i became a supporter.

I can't tell you how gutted I was after putting so much time and effort into getting everything that these committee members could only dreamed of at the time fact. So I took my bans on the chin and at the time I knew they wanted me banned as they knew the club East end Amateurs would fold or just lose everything and fall out of there league. Because as East End never broke any of there rules as a club they couldn't throw them out.

But I kept going to games to watch my brother and friends that played in the team. Lee Cheeser and David Longmuir ran the club. I was only a spectator at council public parks also in new Advocates park which is in closed and is private ground which I was a club member so had every right to be able to watch East End Amateurs when they played at new Advocates park.

I was banned for 2 years after being assaulted by both brothers and even was hit with a hammer yet I never gave any statements that would of got anyone in trouble and the fines prove that as you've read there was children and people everywhere yet they got less punishment than I got. I was summoned to a meeting and I had nothing to do with football.

I got banned for anything and was at Hampden more times than the Scotland side in season 2005-6 for Appeals that at the time were £150 a pop plus petrol money big money when you've appealed 5 times and they keep your money if you lose. But the AAFA chairmen got £150 each month for expenses. Told to me by himself outside Hampden prick so £1800 a year is a half decent week away for him and his misses.

See with all the bands I got in total they tallied up to 7 years there people in jail that's pure sex offenders doing less time. The bans are savage in Amateur football because referees reports means cash for the coffers of the pockets of the committee members for there expenses.

There worse than local MPs Kirsty Blackman for dodge expenses sheets. Am not calling any-one thieves as am on about a committee in charge 14yrs ago.

I had nothing to do with the running of East End amateurs in season 2005-06 but I worked and paid council tax so had every right to be able to stand at a council pitch and watch my brother fact so why they can ban you when all your doing is spectating is beyond me.

I wonder if I would of ended up with a 2 year ban if I had reported him for assaulting me first to the police he would have been Charged for Assault his brother would have been jailed if I hadn't told everyone to say nothing to the police as one thing am not is a GRASS. Think about it this game made the BBC news and as you can read its still there I had all the top Scottish daily national news papers asking for the story but had I spoke about this back then Gary who iv spoke to since would have been jailed had I said he had hit me on the shoulder with the claw hammer and also hit one East End players having him needing medical assistance if ev-eryone had put in statements both would have been jailed not a silly fine so think iv covered that and the Sun star and the daily record all offering money for a lot less reading than this plus I would of jeopardized his court case.

I got banned and wasn't even in the country at the time of one of these under trained referees that cost people there careers with the crazy lying reports that are submitted to these kanga-roo courts you appeal to.

Believe it or not in one of my Appeal meetings one of the disciplinary committee asked me why my passport wasn't stamped when I was on holiday in Spain back in 2005 so that's what your up against why would they stamp your passport coming home from Spain retard simple and they never knew if it was me or my brother that had committed the accused offense in one case the club was involved with I even supplied the hotel telephone number the hole nine yards and still got banned.

The referee honestly couldn't pick out me or my brother. So this is how corrupt the chairman of the AAFA allegedly he showed the referee a picture of myself and made that referee lie all true the man told me himself and a person i know very well and he has nothing to do with football so i defiantly know he wouldn't lie. And iv had a good few others that have told me so they basically knew that if I was out of the way the team would fold. Yet Lee David and my Brother Scott along with others were running that team not me.

They stopped my entire football career because had I only been a player and not player man-ager I wouldn't have got half the ban time I received. So all the successes and effort was all for nothing, because as iv said JEALOUSY at the age of 30.

Season two in the Aberdeen Amateur league went south to say the least. Well we started the new season with both lee and David in charge my youngest brother Scott was helping them both plus playing in goals and taking the training along with all involved with the club done there part. The team was doing really well until we played Woodside Amateurs in February 2006

East End amateurs started the 2nd season at home on New Advocates against Kittybrewster who they beat 1-0 with Dean Davidson getting the goal as Lee and Davie were working with Dean upfront as they had brought in a few new players, on the first game of season and as a club East End still had 8 players in the 16 man team picked by the new management pairing of Lee Davie and my brother Scott taking training so that was his first experience of running a team training session which had set him in good stead as he later on when he had stopped playing so much took over as manager of Rattrays XI and won them there first amateur League trophy since season 1990/91 the club was formed in 1947 and in season 2009/10 there longtime Clubman Billy Allan was crying after the game and as am writing this sadly Billy has past on so RIP Billy and am glad my Brother brought that man some great joy and pride on a great night for all involved with that club. So East End got off to a winning start at there private ground that's a members only working mans club.

They also played one of the big teams of the Aberdeenshire Amateurs Echt in October 2005 in a Scottish cup game and East End had only eleven players that day and were up 2-0 at Half-time and Echt were near the top of the premier League and in the end Echt managed to pull the game back maybe if East end had subs then it might have been a different out come but they ended up knocking East End out of the cup 3-2 in a great game.

Played in great spirit with East End only picking up one booking and Lewis Smith was on the score sheet and Echt tried signing him after the game mad.

That season Echt won the Aberdeen AFC trophy and the Association cup so even in season four the club after all the trouble the club was getting was totally unjustified could you imagine if I had kept a few more player plus myself playing we would of became a force in amateur football as the foundations were all in place and that's what got on the nerves of certain people involved with the AAFA and am not paranoid as you can see as you read on.

The fourth season was going well for the club they were wining games with a few draws and only 3 losses so they played Woodside coming off the back of two draws and a win so the team were playing OK especially at home on the bigger pitch were they could exploit the flanks and get crosses in the box causing these not so fit teams that couldn't handle the teams pace. So the team were away so because back then Woodside used public pitches like where the first game was played at Shedocksley I watched the game from the hill above the pitch well away from the touchline.

So during that game the well known referee who owns a watering hole on Crown street Aberdeen and is friends with old Joe and the things the Woodside players were getting away with was unreal. 10 players booked yes East End players Joe broke one of the East End defenders nose with a clear elbow off the ball that fool of a man cant play just a bully so the team was up against it a muddy small pitch suited Woodside.

As iv said at New Advocates its twice the size of these public pitches so they won 2-0 so there was no hassle and everyone went home apart from Craig who went to get his nose looked at. East End hadn't played same as most clubs due to the winter weather but the club had been training and injured and suspended players were coming back into the team so the club played Johnshaving away and won 7-1 with Club captain Chris Smith got scored one in a great team performance before the club were due to play Woodside in a cup game again at New advocates.

Since the last time the clubs met the manger of Woodside assaulted a completely harmless mentally ill man who is no longer with us RIP, and at the time was close to my middle brother. So me hearing this and knowing how it had affected that defenseless man.

He gave this seriously mentality ill man loads of stitches above both his eyes he look a mess the whole 7 stone of him. So iv a good heart people I could never do what he done and he knew this man for years and a hundred percent that he was very very ill but no he gave him a proper beating. So I was going to have it with him at some point during that game or after as it was a pure Liberty and the man was never the same again proper sin.

So the games at Aulton surprise surprise the Amateur fixture person managed to double book us with the juniors so we had to play at the cat and dog home. So teams make the long walk from the dressing rooms at Aulton to the pitches. Which has had a total revamp since those days pissing of rain dodging traffic with football boots on great. If your not familiar with what it was like there was kids having to make that dangerous trip down to the pitches for years before they done anything to improve the situation.

So match day am nerves because am banned but am not listening to allegedly corrupt money grabbing association who drew us with Woodside in two cups in the space of 3 weeks. Looking back I got pure stitched up by that bunch of jealous old fossils.

So iv turned up at the game with my head having some real proper mad thoughts about what the scenario was going to be as I hadn't slept playing all different things that could happen so My belly is in knots as I knew it was going to go off at some point. East End were all over them and they couldn't have argued if East End beat them 5-1 that day Dean Davidson scored a cracker but missed at least 3 one on ones and they also missed a penalty that being the East End player who got the back of his head opened up with a claw hammer on the touchline he had been substituted for his team mate player Floody from Liverpool who was up here staying due to work in the North east sector and was only on the bench due to the fact he had dislocated his knee against Ellon in the October of the previous year .

Then near the end Woodside equalised to put the cup game into extra time.

We had a good few boys from the team there who were banned or injured so most left when the game went into extra time. As it was one of those great Scottish Aberdeen wind that cuts you in half so it was proper freezing and my middle brother had both his dogs with him as well a English bull mastiff and a English bull terrier letting them get a run about as the pair were great dogs.

So the games a few minutes into extra Time and bang East End score after a great pass by new signing making his debut Fraser black what a game to make your first start. After that Woodside couldn't take getting beat and then a fight broke out between a East End player and the Woodside player manager.

Ending in both being sent off as I had told floody to go on and nail him and take a red as a spectator when he was being put on by whoever in the East End management team as Mcgunigle was spitting on players and proper trying to hurt East End players because his team wasn't good enough when East End hadn't even most of there first team regulars playing like Floody in the center of the park who was a really good player also forward Steven Gribble who had been scoring a few goals but was injured a week before but was at the game and left the same time as my brother as the pitch we were using you could basically park next to the pitch where Gary was sitting in a car watching the game.

I had nothing to do with the running of East End amateurs in season 2005-06 but I worked and paid council tax so had every right to be able to stand at a council pitch and watch my brother fact so why they can ban you when all your doing is spectating is beyond me. I wonder if I would of ended up with a 2 year ban if I had reported him for assaulting me first to the police he would have been Charged for Assault his brother would have been jailed if I hadn't old everyone to say nothing to the police as one thing am not is a GRASS. Think about it this game made the BBC news and as you can read its still there I had all the top Scottish daily national news papers phoning me and Lee had the same thing all asking for the story but had I poke about this back then Gary who iv spoke to since would have been jailed had I said he had hit me on the shoulder with the claw hammer and also hit one East End players having him needing medical assistance if everyone had put in statements both would have been jailed not a silly fine so think iv covered that and the Sun star and the daily record all offering money for a lot less reading than this plus I would of jeopardized his court case.

Then rather than go off the pitch on the Woodside sideline he came off at our side with some children still watching the game the Woodside manger Joe came straight for me as I said it was freezing with one of them winds that cut right through you. I had gloves my hood up and he marched towards me now bear in mind at that point I had court cases coming left right and center due to an ex neighbour trying to take the piss and they done what most in this Aberdeen do is start shit and then when a mad man comes looking to fight back they run to the police.
was sound with him so iv seen most of the people involved and things aren't a problem now well not in my book might be after people read this lol.

But as I was saying Joe has the look iv seen so many times in my life so he's head butted me and iv took my jacket and gloves off and started battling as I was getting the better off him and I was holding the Bullie Woodside Managers boss up and upper cutting the fuck out of him then I felt a sharp pain on the back of my right shoulder. some of his players had a kick at me because I was on my feet during the whole carry on rangers Ryan Jacks brother Stephen was playing in the game he kicked me on the side and knew it was him due to him being the only player with white boots on I met him a few years later he was in my mothers house fixing her boiler and he went white as his boots but I was OK with the lad at the end of the day he was a Joe arse licker.

During this my brother and other team members stood there ground one player used the linesman's flag that we had which was one of the old wooden handled ones to smash the hammer wielding thug as the children on our side line were terrified at such scenes.

Also big David Longmuir gone but not forgot took the hammer from the fat object of a man having to use weapons at a football match. All because his brother was getting smashed about from me easy and I let him hit me first and back then I would of went for it with anyone in this town so there's police cars screaming to the pitches ans as you can see and no Snitches here,so iv been pulled away from the Chaos that was going on but I can swear on my kids life I played it all down to the police and they were treating this serious and wanted team lines were never away from my house but they got nothing from me I told them to see the referee for them as I had nothing to do with the team and told them to stop coming to my house.

So had they got any assistance then there would have been Jail sentences not fines being handed out and what would have been the point in that I proved I could smash his brother even after giving him a free butt and punch at me and as iv said already his brother had to come from the car right next to where I was fighting with his brother with a claw hammer in my

mind I won so why would I need to see someone go to jail where he could of lost everything for a moment of madness it was fair fight between me and Joe apart from Mr Jack with a fly kick but I just went for a beer chilled out went home and spent time with my 2 daughters no hassle as iv said iv been brought up round violence which isn't good to be honest but you play with the hand your dealt its learned me that. Some people reading this might not understand but its just my life and this is only me writing about my football life no my whole life story, and remember everyone has there time.

Aulton Aberdeen Council pitches where the hammer attack took place.

The new Changing Rooms the fighting took plabe behind that new changing Rooms.

After that mad game East End Amateurs team played one more game against Blackburn at there pitch they have had redone so its a nice enough pitch for an amateur side so East End.

No Grasses Here as you see he couldn't be happier.

beat them 1-0 and that was the last game for the club the players were getting sent off for nothing it ended up it was very clear they never wanted East End in there corrupt league so the team left there league and they were trying to fine the club £300 and wanted the club representatives to go to meetings which Lee done and he left knowing it was time to give it up.

Success can be your downfall in all things in life depending on the people who envy you some as you've read they will lie cheat to make sure your not successful so if anything its a life experience you find in business as well as football but as things are with my injuries I might even write about the lot more mad life experience have had In my Colourful life iv lived just this little football stories are unbelievable thankfully iv people that can back my stories up.

Also before I finish about East End Hammers there was a friendly game when a East End Player was Charged for assaulting the same referee who he according to all involved he tapped him smiling saying something in the words of thanks its about time you booked one of there players and yet was brought to court and fined £500 and the club in the local newspaper and maybe national papers for a cheeky very very minor tongue and no pun intended cheeky slap round the face and the opposition manager gave a police statement to the police and bang the East End player has no choice but to plead guilty to the charge.

See this is a town known for grasses that don't understand that what turned from a laugh into a man losing everything [I know its still an assault in the eyes of the law] but it was well over played and that was not only players telling me about it this was people who's friends and family were at the game and the Junior club East End were playing was Dyce and according to the East End people there should have been a junior referee even tho it was a friendly this guy was in his first season as a referee after the game went and asked advice from referee Gary C who was terrible and hated me and told him to get the police why didn't the referee phone the police from the game if he felt threatened since hes just had a slap round the face that's caused him to go home speak with another referee then phone the police.

Well my thing there is if I was this scared for his life referee why didn't he call the police from inside the changing rooms the East End social club which is all one building next to the pitch people so you decide on that one, but as I say one day they will meet there maker and he will decide these deceitful jealous and corrupt peoples destinies.
As for the player he went on and then lost his job and family in part to that liar of a referee who himself is on record of saying as iv wrote this was made to lie and he will one day pay

long with all these other people involved with these bans and unfairly how an ambitious East End was treated terrible while in the AAFA alleged allegations save anyone thinking they can sue me.

Even tho I know you the reader can make your own mind up and for players and coaches that have faced me or any of my teams iv manged we were far from hatchet men or depilatory ever trying to hurt other players iv been guilty of a few missed timed tackles just like the pros on TV and iv held team talks telling the players that certain games that they will need to get stuck in but there's only been one game iv ever told a player to take a red was in the Woodside game due to as iv explained due to the conduct of Woodside player Manager Joe McGunnigle trying to really hurt people and am sure plenty of people over the years of them being in the league have had run ins with that prick.

Here are some of the players playing that fateful day in February 2006.

Captain Christopher Smith.

My experience of playing and being captain of both the Royals FC and East End Amateurs was brilliant playing for player manager Steven Cameron and with in the center of midfield who with his experience of playing junior football he learned me good habits even though I done all the running he was good to play with as he was good at getting me to time when to make runs and when to hold the ball or pass he made me a better player plus I was playing with my long term pals.

To from where we started off too having all the things he promised including us joining up with Junior Club East End so we even had a home junior pitch which back then there wasn't many amateur clubs had which had a decent surface to play on so that was absolutely great and the season was going well until we played that fateful game against Woodside amateurs. From the start we knew it would kick off if we won or were wining the game, low and behold we went 2-1 up in extra time and it went bananas. Personally I just watched the madness from the pitch as I was there to play a game of football.

All in all it was a god dame shame as that was the end of the dream we created from nothing to a solid run amateur club just looking to play a game of Saturday football. This is my honest opinion it was a combination of things but there was people who still thought Steven had something to do with the running of the club when I helped with training along with his brother Scott who we were brought up with lived on the same street and went to the same schools, so me and him were the ones along with David RIP big man and Lee who were basically running the show. But there was definitely some people never liked the fact that dreams can be achieved and we were going in the right direction as a club.

Scott Cameron Goalkeeper.

This my views on my football career I played as goalkeeper from a very young age due to my big brother Steven played since I remember and would sometimes remember go watch him play at the Lads club when my mum would go and watch him play so I got the bug for football.

And would practice everyday for hours with my brother Steven in either the school field or in the back garden he would just take shots at me and crosses if we were in the field so I enjoyed playing in goals and played my first game in goal for Middlefield Primary school aged 10 years old. I could also play upfront and have scored my fair share of goals over the years including while playing for the royals in the last kick of the ball to grab an equaliser.

But I have played junior and in the welfare and at that time if it wasn't my brother running it I would of probably not played at that level but really enjoyed my time playing in the welfare and Amateurs and then when I played junior it was good as well I just wanted a game of football every week.

But that Woodside game wasn't my brothers fault as he was all wrapped up as it was freezing because I wasn't doing much in the game as we could of and should have had the game won well before extra time.

So one of many issues playing for East End Amateurs was this game when it erupted into a massive brawl happened and I ran from my goal as the referee ran past me poor man I just seen my brother fighting back after not like my brother would normally do back then was give someone a couple of free shots at him but due to grasses he was on bail and couldn't hit first or even though he knew Joe was coming straight at him.

He let him as iv said get a couple in then my brother was holding him with one hand and upper cutting him with his other fist and it was just the two then there players got involved and me and most of the team where all in a mealy when his brother Gary then appeared with a hammer hit one of the East End player over the head then my brother over the back.

Now most people reading this would think run but where we were brought up this was normal so there was police vans cars the lot iv never seen so meany and who was they looking for guess who my brother but he was sitting in the East End social club having a pint mad fucker he is I swear he was or me bothered about it yet it mad national news and hes been whipped away by my mate Duncan as you could here the police like it was a fight at Pittodrie.

But I was helping Davie and Lee we all chipped in as a team as most of the players were with the team since our Royals days and I enjoyed playing football with my long term pals, I had a few offers to play junior but enjoyed playing for my brothers team as he came good on all he promised us. Just a great shame the way things turned when we went and played Amateur I was even getting sent off and people that know me am not one for getting red cards, but after I stopped really playing I managed and played now and then for Ratterys XL and won the amateur division 2 league cup there 1st trophy in many years so must of learned something through my 25 years career.

Fraser Black debutant.

What a game for the poor man to make his debut.
Ken never forgot that was fucking mental! Deano scored a peach that day!!

Dan Macrae.

I canna mind much about it mate! Just mind it kicking off and walking back to changing rooms with floody. Ok your not on trial Dan.

Graham will.

I remember Fraser black making hes debut 1 and only appearance, Deano scoring a 30 yard volley beating them in extra time they went down to 10 then lost the plot.

Lee and his son Jordan Chesser 9yr old.

I was totally shocked at what I was seeing and was trying to protect my son jordon as its not something I wanted my 9 year old son seeing what was going on but this is what he remembers from that day he probably will never forget because iv never witnessed that at a football match even on TV. Like to say RIP Davie Longmuir.

I can only remember some bits of it it mind that cunt got sent off and he started walking towards you if I mind write you had a bubble jacket on because it was freezing at day and kinda mind when you was fighting at boy flew out the car we the hammer and hit the East End player over the head with it and you on the back and I was Probably terrified out my skin.

Greg Mcsloy.

Only game I've ever been to in my puff that you could cut the atmosphere with a knife and that was before kick off, played some good football that day before a few dirty tackles came out way followed by a dismissal then a riot, made me proud knowing if I'd gotten in to shit on or off the field my teammates and my pals would have had my back!

Dean Davidson goal scorer.

Yeah that was someday! It was a windy ass cunt of a day. The tension was there even before the game started. Both sidelines constantly swearing at each other, the challenges were flying in from the first whistle. I knew something was going to erupt. I remember going down 1 nil and the tension grew even stronger between the sides.

Not sure who crossed the ball it could of been chewy, I scissor kicked the ball I knew it was in once left my foot the wind caught it and bent it round the keeper. That was it all hell broke lose after he got sent of then he came for you after being sent off the pitch fighting in the middle of the sideline with McGunnigle and then the Brother pulled a hammer out of his van that's all I remember.

Steven Batty Long serving player.

At was some day at was like for me pal I was shocked lost for word and couldn't believe my eyes fit I was seeing we were better team that day think it was extra time we game finishing 1-1 after 90 minutes then I think I hit post just start of first half of extra time before Deano put use 2-1 up then 5/10 minutes after at it just went mentally after at.

I support Aberdeen and the fans that have a go at Stephens brother for leaving Aberdeen for arch rivals Rangers but if another company offered these same people that call him a traitor would do exactly the same triple your wages your going, so see it like that people as that's there job and its not a long career and either is running a team in the AAFA not a long career at all.

The 1st season we entered the league at the same time as Westdyke and they were in the same division as us that season and out at Westhill playing fields not far from Aberdeen football clubs new training facility we played them with a good team and thrashed them 4-1 with me scoring 2 and fellow Striker Craig Murison got the other 2 but I remember we were one nil down and they got a penalty in which would of put them 2 ahead and would of changed the game completely.

So am going mad as it was a stupid clumsy challenge from my center back so there player steps up to take the pen and boom my brother saves the day with a great save, a good keeper will gain you 12 points a season when you analysis your teams performance over the course of a season, here's just one example I know that had the pen went in we might not of won that night but it gave the whole team a lift, Westdyke last time I looked they were still going strong and they beat us 2-1 at New advocates and both clubs were up there with your established teams if not by far better set ups and proper sponsors like we both had.
They made it all the way to the premier league but they are mid table in Division one same league as my friend Andrew Ewen who is Manager of top of the table Kinchorth Amateurs.

So a late friend of mine who was a great man was running an amateur side Sunnybank Amateurs who had great success in previous seasons but for all sorts of reasons they lost a lot of player and had a terrible start to season 2007/08 and I ended up giving him numbers of the players that had played for me at the Royals and East end and in that season they went from struggling at the bottom end of the table to well up the league. I remember one Scottish cup game in Drumchaple in Glasgow the Donald Dewar sports center well since I wasn't allowed to play I went looking for a beer rough old place but cant remember the pub me and injured player Ian Henderson who played for my old team said you mental going in there and I remember his words before we went in please don't hold a carry on great coming from him when hes drunk it was next to a shopping arcade rough joint but no one bothered us and were fine enough people. So both of us missed the start of the match but I do remember the player manager scored a pure belter in the 4-1 defeat which wasn't a real reflection on the game but they were a welcoming team and the bus trip home was funny to say the least.

And as I say there is a lot of work put into running a Football team at any level as you always have players out with injuries suspensions and a big thing in all lower league teams players with work commitments and even back then I would never complain if a player needed to work at times it would piss me off but players have family's and bills to pay and when I was manager I got the best insurance policy the club could afford and I would put money out my own pocket as well to fund things if I needed.

To have training at Strikers for a good few seasons then its costly there's then Northfield Acadamy ASDA Garthdee the university has a place in Craigton road Aberdeen Fc have a place in Kingwells also a place called Goals ok for a kick about but no use for adults training was always a last resort for me. Strikers now that place is a gold mine as there's really a shortage of winter training facilities in the northeast of Scotland so they can charge what they like

nd its just a constant flow of teams using there facilitates because as I say there's not enough
places for the size of the CITY
not TOWN,

Try booking starting from the south to the north of the city, Cove Rangers hire there pitch un-
sure of pricing but they do different formats so they can maximize there profit which any
good business does and whatever Cove are doing its working because there going up the senior leagues with easy and a former team mate of mine at Cuminnstone Dougie Scully who
was a steady player and he got stuck in was a decent player, and he must be so proud for how
well his son has developed over the years to be a first team player for Cove Rangers since
igning in 2013 aged 20-21 years old and is now in his ninth season so knowing his dad am
sure he has had a influence on his son Conner Scully who was just a baby when I played at
Cuminnestone United with his father screaming at me to pass the ball.

Think I drove Dougie crazy and if your reading this my man remember I was a kid when I
was playing but I had ability and I wasted it and I think you seen that and it annoyed you plus
the fact I was a cocky young fucker so that's probably another reason why he always used to
ose it with me but I knew he was a winner and could play but lets just say some of the others
being honest not even good Amateur players never mind junior so when your playing good junior teams they would rip us apart right from the off some games but as iv said when players
like Dougie and George Valentine Ronnie MacDonald Snr would use all his years of experience in the center of the pitch and was still a very fit man for his age and his son Ronnie Jnr
was the same age as me and was also a regular at the back.

Big strong lad got stuck in as well so when as iv said had a squad we would beat or draw with
anyone on our day in the bottom 5-6 clubs there wasn't much between them and if I was on
fire teams like Maud would get beat 4-0 with me getting 2 and my old partner in crime Jim
got a brace that game to. Am sure Dougie son should be grateful because if my father had the
passion for football rather than outdoor sports I might of played at a lot higher level than I
did so well done Dougie am sure your very proud of your son.

Also when you we're a kid you looked at the Junior pitch and dreamed of playing on it. Even
though I had played on Sunnybank Juniors pitch Heathryfold park as a 10 year old here is
the clubs history as over the years its went into a bit of a decline but there making a recovery
nowadays.

Sunnybank Juniors are a <u>Scottish</u> <u>football</u> club, based in the city of <u>Aberdeen</u>. Members of the
<u>Scottish Junior Football Association</u>, they currently play in the <u>North First Division</u>. In re-
spect of honours won, the club are historically regarded as one of the "big two" of <u>North
Region</u> Junior football along with city rivals <u>Banks O' Dee</u>, sharing the distinction of being the
only North clubs to lift Junior football's national prize, the <u>Scottish Junior Cup</u>. The club are
based at Heathryfold Park in the North-West suburbs of <u>Aberdeen</u> and their colours are black
and white. So as you see over the last few years the club like so many junior clubs there running on a shoe string budget.

But they did manage to do something no other Sunnybank team will or any other North East
Junior side win the Junior Scottish cup. This is the history of this once giant of Scottish Junior
Football. Sunnybank FP were founded in 1936 and played in youth football until the onset of
<u>World War II</u>. In 1946 the club merged with another local side Belmont, founded in 1944, and
joined the Aberdeen & District Junior Football League as Sunnybank F.C.. The club won
their first cup competitions in 1947-48, first league championship in 1951–52 and in 1953–54

won the <u>Scottish Junior Cup</u>, defeating <u>Lochee Harp</u> in front of 22,600 fans at <u>Hampden Park</u>, <u>Glasgow</u>, the first club from what would become the <u>North Region</u> to do so

Since 1946 the club had played at Linksfield Stadium, near the centre of <u>Aberdeen</u> but in 1957 purchased the site of Heathryfold Park from Lord Hay of Seaton, a local landowner, for the sum of £360. Although at that time on the city outskirts, the ground was soon surrounded by new housing schemes such as <u>Northfield</u>. This enabled the club to operate a thriving <u>social club</u> although in the early 21st century, this has fallen on hard times.

As a result of winning the 2009–10 <u>SJFA North Superleague</u>, the club earned entry to the <u>Scottish Cup</u> for the first time in their history. On 1 September 2010, Sunnybank were drawn away to <u>Gala Fairydean</u> of the <u>East of Scotland Football League</u>. This tie was played on 25 September 2010 which they won. In the next round, they were drawn **away to <u>Albion Rovers</u> of the <u>Scottish Third Division</u>, and caused a shock by winning 1–0. Their reward in the third round was a match away to <u>Scottish Second Division</u> side <u>Ayr United</u>. However, their run in the Scottish Cup was to come to an end as they were beaten 5–0.**

Owing to the resignation of their management team and a lack of signed players, the club were on the verge of taking a year out in July 2011 with the intention of returning for the start of the 2012–13 season, however they continued after a deal was agreed to use the youth players of local rivals Banks O' Dee.
Just two seasons after winning the league, however, they were relegated to the North Division One after achieving just six points out of 26 games. Their only win was a 3–1 victory at <u>Lewis United</u>.

The team are managed since June 2016 by Keith McHattie. I know Keith from him playing junior at East End so through our East End connection I know him quiet well fine man and hes trying his best at the club but as they say you can only piss with the cock you've got.
In November 2016 the club appointed Gordon Milne as goalkeeping coach. Iv also played at East End with Manager Keith Mchattie.

But Sunnybank aren't the only North Junior side to win the Scottish cup. Banks O' Dee's greatest achievement was winning the Scottish Junior Cup in 1957, defeating Kilsyth Rangers 1–0 in the final at Hampden Park, Glasgow in front of 30,800 spectators.

Aberdeen FC would be delighted with a crowd like that considering there average attendance is about 13k for home games how times have changed.

There will never be another North of Scotland Junior club win the Scottish cup again unless it becomes like Amateurs due to lack of money and the bigger junior clubs leaving and joining other teams into the pyramid system which is a great thing for Scottish football.

And it's far to long in happening as it's improving the lower senior teams. football and it's far to long in happening as it's improving the lower senior teams because if they don't they find themselves relegated unlike before where season after season the same teams came bottom of the third division year after year and the lower bottom half of the league became a joke iv played on better playing surfaces at junior level than some of the bottom Scottish clubs facilitates are or were shocking big junior and some highland league and south lower league have far better playing surfaces and facilities.

Even when I played junior at a young age I always thought these teams had far better grounds than the teams coming bottom year after year. So am all for ambitious

clubs moving forward as it's good for the game. I know people go on about clubs history's and things well improve and your club won't get relegated or if that's all ready the case try get back in the league and there's only one way of doing that and it's improving the whole club. Which is good for the game I do think the government should be investing more into these smaller clubs rather than spend money on two or three all weather surfaces for the kids just to play on and there's no lighting in the winter nights why not give it to these junior and lower league clubs the surfaces and make sure it's available for all to use when the club has no game.

That would also mean semi-professionals and Amateur clubs would not be playing on council owned terrible pitches. And there would be less of a fixture build up. Just look at Sunnybank that club is on deaths door as a social club compared with years gone by and with the size of the actual social club all these facilities could be being used on a nightly basis if there was a artificial surface and floodlights the pitch could be there for use every night and would give the youth clubs a place to train and not have games off due to Scottish weather I know there's a pitch at Northfield Academy but that isn't enough for the size of the area of Northfield also Mastrick plus there's a perfectly good swimming pool lying closed and there's a school there teach the kids to swim because teaching them that mans been to the moon isn't any good if they fall in water.

Bonus Stories and Pictures

These are all mixed stories, I played at Cuminnestone United with former Sunybank juniors manager Tommy McPherson who was a decent player but just wanted a game like myself but we did clash on the pitch but after the game things would be brand new and at training we would take the piss out of some of the other boys you know what like the banter is at teams if you have played team sports you will understand. See when I was a younger man I knew if I would get on with some teams just by telling the type of banter there is at the club was the reason I left Hall Russell's was due to the dressing room every week pure silence among the players where even at Eat End Juniors when I signed after Cuminnestone United folded and Andy went there and as I mentioned the unrest in the dressing room its hard when you suffer from a mood disorder and self doubt and anxiety being in these situations are daunting and for me as iv said could tell after being at training or in the dressing room weather I wanted to stay at that club and if you've played team sports you will understand what I mean you feel the mood of the other players if there's a bad vibe I was off especially when the team was full of cunts speaking about each other, see when your new players will ask you what position do you play your like relax am 2 minutes in the door and there's cunts worried for there place and you haven't even kicked a ball yet Junior football is mad, well that East End Dressing room was ok between some players then you had this other group who never wanted

Andy there as manager so that's why I left I couldn't be done with the politics I was having to sit listening to from players who never knew I personally knew Andy. But with me and Tommy we and the rest of the players at Cuminnestone United all wanted the same thing, just a game on a Saturday and if we were up against one of the bottom 5-6 clubs we had a chance. With me being the teams best forward player as my goals scoring record as a young boy really at 16-18 years old 24 goals is a great return for a club playing junior football with different players every few games.

So me and Tommy clashed to start with because he was older but he then became friends because even when i was a young man I could look after myself and both of us used to get a good laugh then he left after the club folded so that's how I ended up meeting Tommy and what he done with his Sunnybank team was a great feat.

Tommy managed Dyce Juniors for a bit but I think due to family commitments he had to pack the game in. Dyce will never win the super league because they don't sign Roy kean type players simple if you show your frustrations and get excited like I get at times just like Tommy is he calls a spades a spade for when your dealing with Tommy at football this is no bad reflection on either Tommy or Dyce as a club.

This is all about football and doesn't reflect on peoples everyday life so don't think am having a go at anyone about there all round personality as people change at football like most sports people get in the zone and lose the plot at times but that's football when its all done and dusted most people are different people when there in the pub win or lose, if you lose its home depressed think what went wrong why do you think am able to write this because I was passionate to win and as iv said I thought the team reflected on my personality so that's why I was determined that the team would have the best possible for the players to show what they could do and when I got banned as these horrible jealous people that run the league back then hated my ambition for the club,

We got also the opportunity to move up and use the East End junior facilities as the club as iv said never had a penny when we joined them and we helped clean the place up and we had nights to raise money between us and the juniors.

When the East End amateurs went under my brother and Lewis Smith signed for the juniors then my brother went for free to Banchory and East End ended up nearly having to pay them a fee to get him back but the only reason they got him back for free was due to Banchory not living up to a lot of promises that they failed to live up to and that's why my brother left Banchory.

Plus East End had appointed Allan Keith and his brother Gary who knew my brother from begin his Manager at Middlefield plus he had seen him pay for my teams in friendlies iv spoke about so Allan knew Scott and needed a goalkeeper but Scott was at Banchory playing weekly as the new manager had been assistant at Hermes where Scott had played for and when work started to come first as his family started to grow he left Hermes due to work at that time but had went to Banchory due to knowing there newly appointed manager who had been the assistant manager at Hermes.

And that was the reasons he signed for Banchory was because he knew the new manager. I stood on there side line after paying my money to enter there matches the same as at every junior club my brother played for while I was banned and no amateur league treasurer turned up and alleged I was running there teams or being part of there clubs so you think am paranoid now because what I was doing while being banned was watching my brother to give me something to do on a Saturday.

Yet when he was at East End amateurs as iv said I got banned for watching my brother and friends simple because why did the rules change when he was at junior clubs and I went and paid to watch didn't have the amateur treasurer sneaking about weirdo beside dressing rooms seeing if am taken half time team talks so I would get banned ?

But standing on the Banchory sideline was fun the new manager never stood a chance there was back stabbing people within that club so there was an atmosphere I could even sense from the sideline that he wasn't going to be given a chance yes the manager so when my brother left it wasn't long till they sacked the manager.

This is another true story I was playing in the summer league at Sheddocksley sports fields for a friend at the time Neil Stewart great man had a good juvenile side himself but just he was unfortunately playing in the same league as Allan and Gary Keith's Juvenile sides I mentioned earlier in the story so anyway.

Neil called be maybe half an hour before kick off saying he was struggling for players that night so I managed to get my middle Brother Andrew to help out that night, but I had bought a new pair of boots that day as the pitches were solid at that time of year so the games started referee Sandy Flett who will testify to this story along with at the time my kids mums cousins boy friend who was from the Hilton area so he had came to watch the game as he knew some of the younger players and also myself and my brother so as you know as the legs get older and the pitches are rock solid plus the I had scored a brace my new boots were killing my feet so as the game was well out of reach for our opponents I decided to say to Neil since we were winning and there was a couple of substitutes.

So iv sat down took off my boots and socks and remember there's not been a booking in this game never mind any sign there would be what then happened am lying having a joint that was being smoked on the sideline as iv found over the years that herbal Cannabis is good for stopping my thoughts racing and I can concentrate a lot better than when am not smoking it like when I was working offshore I never touched it but that's another story I could do another follow up if anyone enjoys these ups and downs iv suffered in just my football life.

So as I was saying someone had a joint and I was chilling watching the game when my brother Andrew is running shoulder to shoulder a race for the ball when my brother and the other player are both running when my brother falls and the opposition teams player just lost the plot completely and kicked my brother full force in the face while hes trying to get to his feet, well you don't need to know what happened next am on the pitch bare foot punching lumps out this fool who for no reason what so ever thought he would take a free kick at my bro face for no apparent reason so Sandy has done one am now chasing this big ball bag all over the pitch as hes looking for his team mates for help and some knew who I was and just thought fuck it pal this is the summer league am not looking on a punched in the face because even his own team mates and management could see clearly that there player was fully to blame and the ball bag wouldn't come back to the changing rooms yet he kicked my bro like he was taking a penalty for no reason at all, I tried getting team lines to wait on him to leave his house for work or wait till the dark nights and was seriously going to hurt him.

You may think that's mad and am not right but in my world you cant watch someone think because he was a big boy that he could just kick my brother full force in the head and could of seriously injured or killed him and would of carried on his attack if I hadn't punched him silly and another runner but believe me he was a bully and picked on the wrong man simple or he would of thought he was the alpha male and would of dished out a kicking on a defenseless man trying to get to his feet and start playing a game of football.

But trouble just follows me and here's what dean who I still speak to give you his memory's of the event. I just remember your brother trying to get up and the boy smashed your brother full blast in the face then you were up in seconds on the pitch punching fuck out the boy in your bare feet funny and the referee done a runner and the boy ran and you waited on him for ages I think you even went into there changing room asking for the team lines to see where he stayed mad man but it wasn't you who started that.

I worked with Ray Stephen Dundee 1980-87 playing 181 games scoring 47 and French side Nancy 1987-91 playing 152 games scoring 55 signed by Arsene Wenger after he spotted him at a friendly tournament and signed Ray from Dundee who's from Aberdeen but wasn't good enough for Alex Ferguson but Arsene Wengers seen goals and only paid £175k its crazy to think they ended up both challenging for the English premier league and Ray was working with me at Swire great guy and has some cracking stories like here's just one he told me at his time at Dundee FC there was a player that ever morning run they done he would win no problem and the club had a old tea earn in the dressing room this is back in the 80s when sports science wasn't the best to say the least well Rays team mate he would always be standing with no pants on and cup of tea in hand and a big smile. Well later on after months of this he told Ray that he was putting his pants in the tea earn. Celtic tried signing Ray he told me in 1989 Billy McNeil called his agent and told him about there interest. He was on more than double that wages at Nancy yes a club that size were paying more than double folks than a club the size of Celtic offered £900 a week and a Scotland Cap poor show.

After my 7 year was completed an old friend was running a team called Scotstown Rovers and the had been struggling a bit just like my life at the time I was basically bordering on the edge of a cliff due to drinking most days as I wasn't having a good time I also had a bad bad cocaine habit this is how bad I was my friend was short of players and had a game out at Kingswells and I cant remember the other teams name but I had agreed to help him out and I had to lines of cocaine in my car before I went into the changing rooms and this is me who suffers from anxiety when going into new dressing rooms but when drugs take over you don't care.

So in I go and I was just sitting there looking about me and thinking they all know am flying and that was the one and only game iv ever took drugs before as my anxiety levels were going through the roof sitting there and there was a weary silence as you get sometimes when there's a few new players come into a team remember iv not trained with this team nothing just got a call asking me to play and iv agreed probably out my skull at the time so the team gets picked and I ended up getting picked to play upfront and I went there thinking iv not played football for seven years and I would be substitute no am flying out my nut iv not played as iv said for years and am on a pitch away to try play football, but I did say if I don't score am throwing my boots in the bucket so the game starts and I chip the goalkeeper after I ran onto a short pass back so the boots came home and we won the game 6-3 in a game we were 4-0 up in so i knew they couldn't defend because you wont score 6 every week so because I played well enough as I had been training at the gym when I wasn't getting completely out my skull so the manager who used to go to secondary school with convinced me to play again.

Well was the next game not against my Local pub team they sponsored Byron well on the Friday night I was in the pub winding up my old school friend Jim Christie and Davie Milne who run the team and I was asking them for a bet that I would score. They never took the bet even though I cant mind getting home I managed to get myself motivated enough to go to the game and what happened I scored as usual so that's the reason they never took the bet because even though I was a fat alcoholic cocaine junkie when am on a football pitch iv a knack of hitting the net. But looking back now I really cant believe I took drugs before a game of football just shows what the power of addition can do but I could write a million page book on that and how I beat my addictions and still fight Daily with my inner demons.

AND REMEMBER GOOD GUYS ALWAYS COME LAST PLUS TIMING IS EVERY-THING IN LIFE AND EVERYONE AND THING HAS ITS TIME,

These clubs are dying before Covid so how must they be feeling.

The Sunnybank Social club and pitch entrance

Formartine United Stand since stepping up to the Highland League Ground Capacity 1800

Ex Junior Club Inverurie JFC now home of Conloy Park JFC.

The Village of Cuminestone 6 miles from Turriff some great Memories playing for them

That Stands been there since first played junior and I scored on that pitch in a 4-1 Defeat.

One of the best players to play in the Scottish football league feel blessed iv seen such great players playing Scottish football. Only Aberdeen's Peter weir could play like him and toy with defenders.

Eoin Jess.

The only this this man has done was be picked for the team of the 90s only because he done some keep ups on the byline against Rangers. Got to be one of the most over rated Scottish players of the 90s.

Born in the village of Portsoy in Aberdeenshire, Jess began his career in Glasgow as a trainee striker at Rangers (alongside future Scotland team-mate John Spencer) but was allowed to leave in 1987; he soon moved back to his home region, signing for Aberdeen. Having made his debut at the end of the 1988–89 season, 18-year-old Jess made an impact in the first team from the outset of the following campaign, starting against Rapid Vienna in the UEFA Cup and against Rangers in the 1989 Scottish League Cup Final at Hampden Park, which Aberdeen won 2–1 The club finished runners-up in the Premier Division, and Jess picked up another winner's medal as an unused substitute in the **1990 Scottish Cup Final**. In 1990–91 he scored 13 league goals and linked up with Hans Gillhaus to great effect as Aberdeen missed out on the title on the final day.

The strikes including a away to **Dundee United,**four away to and three across two home wins over **Celtic**. He won the PFA Scotland Young Player of the Year award for the season. Although Jess played 42 games in 1991–92, the season was a disappointment as Aberdeen finished only 6th in the league. He scored in a September victory over Rangers at Ibrox Stadium which proved to be Aberdeen's last win at that venue until 2017.

1992–93 brought an improvement as the club were league runners-up and reached both cup finals. Jess scored the winning goal in the semi-final of the 1992–93 Scottish League Cup against Celtic and played all 120 minutes of the final which ended in a 2–1 defeat to Rangers.

In March 1993 he suffered a fractured ankle in the quarter-final of the 1992-93 Scottish Cup against Clydebank but was rushed back to fitness after only two months out and appeared as a substitute in the final of the competition, which Aberdeen again lost 2–1 to Rangers.

Despite failing to win any trophies and missing part of the season with his injury, he won the PFA Young Player award for a second time.

In 1993–94 Jess helped Aberdeen to another second-place finish in the Premier Division. He also scored five goals in four matches in the Cup Winners' Cup, finishing joint-top scorer in the competition. The next season almost ended in relegation for the club and Jess started only 15 league games due to a persistent foot injury.

He returned as a regular starter in 1995–96 playing in a more withdrawn central midfield role to accommodate strikers Dodds, Booth and Shearer. He produced an impressive performance in the semi-final of the League Cup as Aberdeen overcame Rangers, scored a long-range goal in a league game against the same opponents a few weeks later and was in the team which won the 1995 Scottish League Cup Final, beating Dundee.

Following this victory, he decided to seek a new challenge in his career and requested a move with his contract due to expire. As he had impressed in Europe against Italian opposition (Torino), Serie A clubs showed an interest and Jess has stated that Sampdoria were keen to sign him un-der the Bosman ruling at the end of the season,

But he was determined that Aberdeen should receive a transfer fee, therefore agreed to a £2 million transfer to Coventry City of the English Premier League in February 1996.

He left Aberdeen for the first time having made 253 official appearances for the club, scoring 63 goals, and the transfer fee they received for him was a record amount.

Me and Royals Captain Christopher Smith with the clubs first ever Cup win the

John Kilminster Trophy.

The Team of the 90s

Wonder how much a team like that would cost today in the crazy prices being played for players.

Aberdeen beach front where iv done many runs along there from where the picture starts to the end and back is a good run. But running on concrete is bad for your joints in the long term so me I would run on the sand jog one run one also balmedie beach is a great place for pre season training been sick a few times out there be-lieve me the hills up and down a good few times and you feel it if like me did no training in the off season. So there's loads of great places in Aberdeenshire to do training in the summer nights but then it gets expensive for all clubs for the limited facilities as iv mentioned,

Balmedie Beach

This beach still has old WW2 bunkers all along the beach so for those who aren't aware of the history of the Aberdeen beach bunkers hers just some of the history of Aberdeen's part in the war.

Balmedie (Scottish Gaelic: *Baile Mheadhain*) is a large village in Aberdeenshire in Scotland. It lies north of the city of Aberdeen, in the civil parish of Belhelvie. The long and wide beach is bordered by an extensive dune system that stretches 14 miles (23 km) from Aberdeen to just north of the Ythan Estuary at Newburgh. The dynamic dunes has marram grass as the principal vegetation. They support a large array of wildlife. Two watercourses make their way to the sea within the area creating ribbons of wetland vegetation along their course. The village is near the Sands of Forvie Site of Special Scientific Interest, the fifth largest sand dunesystem in Britain; this is an integral part of the Ythan Estuary, which separates the sands from Balmedie beach.

The Beach at Sunset

Been Sick ruining up them in the past

The Stewart Park in the Rosehill area of Aberdeen this is where we would train in the summer months as the Royals. Great big park where there used to be a cricket pitch and the old Pavilion is still there but is used by the council for people doing community service so it a good clean park there also crazy golf and tennis courts in the park but as for everything in Aberdeen its left to rack to ruine and they wonder why no one uses it crazy but that's councils for you. The park has some great Granite features as well here's some pictures of the things iv spoke about and some history about the park.

Opened in 1894, Stewart Park was named after the then Aberdeen Lord Provost, David Stewart. The area was Land acquired from the Hilton Estate and was designed to be used by all ages. Three disused Quarries were filled in and landscaped as small Lakes stocked with fish. Mrs Taylor, a Widow of a Wood-side Merchant, left £500 to the Park, especially for the purpose of becoming the Taylor Play ground for Children, in memory of her husband. Mrs Taylor was honoured with the Memorial Fountain by the Aberdeen Town Council. Although the Park does not now have the small Lakes, and fewer Flower Beds than when it 1st opened, it is still widely used, and as stated by the Lord Provost at the opening ceremony '*It would be a thing of joy and beauty forever*' to the people *of Woodside*." Soon after the opening of Stewart Park, Cricket Clubs were formed. The Park was home to many Clubs, and memories of the Park suggest that as many as 20 games of Cricket would be in Play at any one time. These

Games obviously paid off because Woodside Cricket Club won the Aberdeen-shire Cup in 1957. Other popular pursuits were the Woodside Football Club, the Grandholm Choir and the *Woodside & District Cycling Club*. The Cycling Club began in the early 30's, but had to disband during WW2. After the War, Joe Dunn, a Cycle Shop Owner and a previous Member, tried to restart the Club

Some great granite work must of took awhile

The Granite fountain

Park Entrance.

This Park was named after the then Lord Provost of Aberdeen, Sir David Stewart. The Hilton & Woodside Amenity was Officially opened on the afternoon of Saturday 9th June 1894. *The Aberdeen Journal's* report of the Ceremony has the Provost responding to a toast by stating *"he did not know what the Park was to be called"*. It was rather hard lines that he should be put in the position of saying 'No' to the request that had been made, but if he had been properly consulted – he would have advised them not to call it the Stewart Park. He might have possibly been pleased about it being called the Stewart Park, and taken a good-natured smile, but he did not think he ever gave his consent anyway. He felt it would be just as well perhaps if the committee called it 'Hilton' or 'Woodside,' and perhaps they would reconsider it. He left the matter in the hands of the Town Council and the name stood.

David Stewart was born in Aberdeen in July 1835, the eldest son of John Stewart and Mary Irvine. David was educated at Rev Dr Gearge Tulloch'sAcademy, Academy Steet, (off Dee Street), Graduated from King's College, Aberdeen in 1855 and joined his father's Comb-making Business. In the 1861 Census David Stewart (25), Comb Manufacturer was residing at Carden Place, Aberdeen with his wife Margaret (24) and 2 Domestic Servants. By 1871 David Stewart (35) Master Comb-maker, had moved to 259 Union Street, Aberdeen, with his wife Margaret (34) and 5 children. For the next 20 years David, in addition to running the Comb Manufacturing Business, played a full Public Role. His list of achievements include:

1883-84 President of Aberdeen Chamber of Commerce
1885-88 Member of the School Board
1885-89 Dean of Guild
1889 Elected to Aberdeen Council as Councillor for Ferryhill Ward
1889-1900 Member of University Court
1889-1895 Lord Provost
1896 Knighted
1891 -1919 Director of Great North of Scotland Railway
1904-1919 Chairman of Great North of Scotland Railway

We used that park to train most weeks when we were the Royals FC also sometimes when we were East End Amateurs as we had the keys to the changing rooms there so when we joined them we mainly trained down the beach area. But our biggest cost was always getting affordable training faculties and not even affordable just trying to get a peak time slot anywhere was hard and if your trying to win and challenge for trophy's you first need a team of decent players willing to win that's the first thing you need then you need sponsors basically running a non league team is hard enough as your doing most things like this getting a permanent train slot for winter. Running an Amateur club is hard at junior level your the management team for the team you shouldn't have to be doing things like trying to get places to train as most well run clubs have a load of committee members and should have some form of lighting for training in the long Scottish months. We used loads of places to train as we were a club trying to compete and win things and the costs were crazy and that was 15 years ago strikers in Bridge of don £70 for 55 minutes on there 7 aside pitch and £45 or £50 for the 5 aside pitches we also would arrange friendlies if games had been postponed for weeks due to the weather then I would try getting a pitch like the university pitch up at HillHead they would only charge £70 for the for 2hrs but it was difficult getting a spot as they came before anyone but here are some pictures of the places in Aberdeen that you can train in the winter.

Hillhead the University's junior teams pitch but they also have an all weather surface as well. Scored on that pitch a few times was first the

home of Bon Accord Juniors and since theres been a few clubs used it until the university bought it and loaned it out to Junior clubs but as iv just said they now have a Junior club of there own.

Strikers £5o for 55 minutes and that was years ago so not sure of the prices now.

Goals

More University Facilities the sports village indoor pitches above and the home of Lewis United Juniors and athletics facilities so as you see the university has great facilities indoor and outdoor.

Northfield Academy and Kamhill Garthdee

Spain Park Banks o Dee Ground Capacity 2300.

Aberdeen's other Junior club who have won the junior Scottish cup and have great facilities and have applied to join the Highland league but failed. But am sure with the new pyramid system now in place and clubs like Cove Rangers FC leaving the Highland league and other leagues around Scotland are going to have to go with the times and allow clubs with the Ambition to move up the leagues should be allowed as it will improve the all round level of football.

Balmoral Stadium New home of Cove Rangers who for years tried and failed to join the senior leagues and have hit the ground sprinting so well done. Ground Capacity seated 370 with a total of 2602.

See what iv noticed since writing this there are far more community based places south of the city than the North as you can see for yourself as there is more poverty North of the city so you would think the councilors would sort the problem iv highlighted a few.

But they just say there's no money bullshit we live in the oil capital of Europe and yet there's still proper poverty and you have people screaming for independence yet the money the council gets isn't being managed correctly if the council which is a business just they are wasting the tax payers money and not there own.

As iv said there definitely needs more money spent on sports to get the kids active but not just active when there young you want people to have the places to go to keep health and then it saves millions later on when these people who enjoyed a sport as a child yet when there an adult there's not the facilities.

And they need to teach the kids about the food chain and how exercise and a proper healthy active life beats any anti depressant iv had enough so an well versed on speaking about depression and how I beat it all my life iv tried to keep myself fit by playing sports or just getting the head phones in and off for a run to clear your head and any stress your under iv found that running is the best way to get fit in my life.

There's no better feeling than when your fit and healthy and me now being incapacitated is driving me insane so never to your health for granted because believe me you don't know how bad it hurts physically but mentally its so hard that your head wants to go for a run yet your physically unable do you know how frustrating that is.

But never mind me so as I was showing you clubs with ambition now in Scotland can move up through the leagues and can only improve the whole of Scotland's football.

Aberdeen Football Club have really messed up with there new stadium with average crowds under 15k and Aberdeen is a very cold place in the winter and they go and start building a new 20k all seated stadium why.

Whoever planned it why didn't they think 15k is great full most weeks and have a retractable roof and think of your loyal supporters who pay there money at the gate week in week out yet come winter there going to be sitting in the snow watching St Mirren.

Then come Rangers or Celtic they may need 17-18k 4 times a season and then these supporters and am guilty of it myself when any of these two clubs come to town I would try get a ticket for the game. Yet if it was a St Johnson you could give me the ticket free and I wouldn't go because the team aren't worth wasting a Saturday afternoon.

Aberdeen are still the first team I look for when am checking the results its just years and years of proper shit football on offer you lose interest. But again that is still a kick back from the madness iv wrote about earlier.

Am glad I seen the player iv mentioned live but its took over two decades for the clubs outside the top two to relise that there never going to compete financially all the smaller clubs are shopping for players in oxford and rangers and Celtic are shopping in Harrods it true so why didn't Aberdeen think of there fans in the winter plus they could have had all sorts of thing if they had a roof pure stupidity in my opinion but never mind its a nice looking Stadium Kingsford Park.

The two things I think need changing is get the kids back playing 11 aside fom age 9 upward needs to be 11 aside so kids can learn early where they should be on the pitch and there positioning as the real game is 11 aside not 7-9 or whatever there playing now. Learning where to be on the pitch is just as important as being able to do a hundred keep ups.

Kids who play football get enough touches of the ball while playing with there friends and play smaller games at training but they must go back to having screaming parents on the sideline and have medals for the kids to win at the end of the season. And your coaches will also be learning more tactical things as well. But for people who haven't seen Kingsford Stadium new home of Aberdeen Football club.

Kingsford Stadium Capacity 20k

Aberdeen's New Home.

Well that's all folks hope you enjoyed the read and I dedicate this book to a friend who past away far too soon David Longmuir.

The reasons this book is being dedicated to David is due to the fact he was a man of his word when it came to getting sponsors for the club was unbelievable. I would say it would be better for the team if we had say better training footballs and I would turn up at training and there would be a dozen new training balls. He was a quite man till that game with Woodside after Choco being hit and me on my shoulder Davie boy went straight at him along with Ian Henderson who got the claw Hammer off Gary the Hammer. But David was also my neighbour and we became very good friends and it was a shock when I found out he had past away. My true opinion of Davie was a man that was desperate to learn about the game of football and was a valuable member of our club and was always listening to what was going on in the back ground. But as iv said your sadly missed my man.